YORKSHIRE AND BACK

YORKSHIRE AND BACK

THE AUTOBIOGRAPHY OF
RAY ILLINGWORTH

written in association with Don Mosey

Queen Anne Press
Macdonald Futura Publishers
London

Filmset by Northumberland Press Ltd, Gateshead,
Tyne and Wear
Printed in Great Britain by
Richard Clay (The Chaucer Press) Ltd,
Bungay, Suffolk

CONTENTS

1
MY CHILDHOOD

Living and growing up in a row of terraced houses is not nearly
as bad as some sociologists and planning authorities would have
us believe. At least, it wasn't during my childhood. There was
a natural community spirit even if none of us thought about it
or put it into words. There was no need to search for someone
to join in a game; a glance through the window would soon show
whether anyone was available. Even if there appeared to be
nobody, one had only to walk out into the street and a football
or cricket team would very quickly materialise.

We all knew each other intimately. Our parents knew one
another. Our brothers and sisters were friends. That was where
we all belonged and our association with each other was simply
a fact of life. We had our close friendships and we had our rivalries,
but ultimately we were all part of the same team. I don't see this
today as a feature of life in high-rise flats, and even in ground-level
urban and suburban developments the sense of unity seems to
have disappeared. Maybe the call of the telly is stronger than that
of the playing field; maybe kids just do not have the same sense
of involvement with each other. Whatever the reason, I think
children growing up today are less satisfied and less contented
than we were.

Perhaps we were just easier to please. All we asked was a place
to play our games – cricket or football, or more elaborate and
esoteric exercises involving one half of the community hiding and
the other half setting out to find them. It was certainly less expensive than skate-boarding, and even today it seems to me a lot more
fun. It is not such a far-fetched idea to feel that my childhood
had a major influence on my passionate involvement with team
games and on my philosophy that no individual is greater than

either the team or the game. On our playing fields we were dependent upon the boy who owned the bat and the one with the ball. Yes, *the* bat and *the* ball. Not many families were affluent enough to provide their children with all, or even more than one, of the accessories, so we were in the hands of the lucky ones with the gear. On the other hand, they needed the rest of us to provide a game – so despite the inevitable squabble from time to time, things worked out on a generally reasonable basis.

My very first recollection of any significant event in my life is of a collision with an extremely substantial stone wall. Yorkshire is liberally equipped with stone walls, all of them extremely solid, and this particular one was outside the first school I ever attended before I was five years old. In a state of wild excitement one day, I rushed out of the school, across the road, and straight into the wall.

My four-year-old consciousness suffered a nasty shock and my four-year-old forehead an even nastier graze. More important than that, it was obviously registered in my subconscious that rushing into something without thought was a particularly daft thing to do, and could result in painful consequences. The memory of that lesson has always remained with me. Many years later, Norman Harris, writing a feature for the *Sunday Times* which contrasted the personalities of Brian Close and myself, asked a friend of both of us how he would have reacted to serving in the trenches with each of us in turn as his commanding officer. This was the considered verdict: 'Closey, without a single glance to see whether anyone was following, would leap over the top and charge at the enemy regardless of odds, the disposition of troops and guns, and without a thought about whether there was cover. Illy would call for a full intelligence report on the enemy's strength and positions, a detailed survey of the terrain between us, an up-to-date report from the Met Office, a final check on the men and weapons of his own forces and then would probably decide against going because the odds were wrong.' That anecdote more or less sums up the difference between Brian and myself, if in rather picturesque terms. Certainly it reflects our characters. I often wonder how much of my reserve and natural caution has been due to that collision with a Yorkshire wall.

While I like to think that I have never been a bad mixer, it is equally true that I have enjoyed close friendship with relatively few people. I have always been basically shy. When I first started going out with Shirley, who became my wife, I would buy a copy of the *Yorkshire Sports* before going up to her parents' home on Saturday evenings and then read it so that I didn't have to get involved in conversation. On a cricket or football field it was different. I felt at home there. I was with people who talked the same language and self-expression came quite naturally in every way. When I became captain of Leicestershire, and then of England, I had to talk formally to journalists and to radio and television interviewers, and initially that was something of an effort. In casual conversation, it was no problem. I have been told I gave pressmen who travelled with Yorkshire 'many an ear-bashing', as one of them put it – but to talk formally, for publication so to speak, was not so easy. However, gradually it became less of an effort and in my years as England captain I even grew to enjoy the interviews. It was gratifying to be able to explain exactly what we had been trying to do and to clear up any misunderstandings which might have been in the minds of some people. Not everyone, unfortunately, sees a game of cricket the same way!

I was born in Pudsey on 8 June, 1932 – during the bodyline era – and automatically I became heir to a great cricketing tradition. That began with 'Long John' Tunnicliffe, opening batsman and slip-catcher extraordinary, who, with J. T. Brown, set up a record first-wicket partnership of 554 in 1898. The tradition continued with Herbert Sutcliffe – although not actually born in Pudsey, he was in every way a Pudsey cricketer – who broke that record in 1932 when he and Percy Holmes scored 555 for the first wicket at Leyton. Then there was Major (first name, not a military rank) Booth, who played for Yorkshire before World War I, and Sir Leonard Hutton, every Yorkshire schoolboy's hero in my generation. I was just six years old when he was scoring 364 against the Australians at The Oval. Could I possibly have dreamed that thirteen years later I would be playing alongside him? There was Herbert Sutcliffe's son, Billy, who might have achieved more in cricket than he did if it had not been for the crippling double burden of being the great man's son and bearing the forenames of William Herbert Hobbs! There was Harry Halliday, too, whose career with the county overlapped mine by two or three years.

Their achievements were my inheritance; their glory was my legacy.

My first bat was made for me by my father in his joiner's workshop. It was unsprung, and I have no doubt it was a trifle coarsegrained: but I loved it. To possess one's own personal cricket bat in the 1930s of the depression-ravaged West Riding was a rare distinction.

When I was only four, the family moved from Pudsey to Farsley, a distance of no more than three miles. West Riding people were not ones for ambitious travel; they liked to be amongst their own folk! My cricket field was the school playground in Frances Street, Farsley, where the stumps were chalked on the wall of the school and a straight six cleared a sweet shop just outside the yard. I didn't play truant and I was never late – because the time before school could be spent playing, seasonally, either cricket or football, and these were the most important things in life to me. My approach was not one of burning fanaticism; that would have been as out of character as any form of extravagantly-expressed enthusiasm is today. It was a simple act of faith. I could think of nothing which could possibly give me more pleasure than playing games. I had no great devotion to academic work, though I had no positive dislike of it, either. No doubt I was reasonably intelligent because there was never any major problem about school work, and I was round about third or fourth in the class when the time came to move on to the next stage of education.

It was at Frances Street School that my sporting roots were first put down. One of the masters, Teddy Shepherd, said one day, 'Every time I come out into the yard it seems to be you who is batting'. So he decided to do something about it, by bowling underhand leg-breaks and googlies to me. Well, this immediately added a new dimension to the game of cricket. In our own game everyone just bowled as fast as possible; the subtleties of swerve and spin were quite unknown to us. But here was something entirely different – hidden menace, disguised threat, something that required thought rather than merely a reaction. For the first time I began to learn something about defensive batting, and I was conscious of gaining a new pleasure from the game.

At the age of eleven, one had to move on to the next stage of education and this was the time to think about sitting a scholarship for entrance to grammar school, if one had ideas in that direction. I hadn't. It wasn't that I disliked school work; in fact I quite enjoyed it, without tackling it with unusual zeal. But sitting a scholarship meant homework, and if I got to grammar school that meant even more homework. That was a matter on which I had very definite views. Homework simply meant an unwarrantable intrusion upon one's spare time, and some curtailment of the hours available for sport: and *that* did not appeal to me one little bit.

So I did not sit the scholarship examination. I said to my parents, 'Look, if I pass it's going to mean homework, more homework and more homework'. Looking back, perhaps they were wrong to agree to my missing the exam, but on the other hand my father may have been much more far-sighted than I was. Perhaps he saw that I had the ability to make a professional sportsman. If he did, then he was very far-sighted, but I just don't know. All I was interested in was making sure that I had enough time to devote to doing the things I loved best in life. That was short-sighted of me, and I am extremely conscious of how lucky I have been for things to work out so well. Cricket has rewarded me generously for the love I gave it. Because I have never been a demonstrative sort of person it may have seemed that my approach to the game has been a little intense. I don't think I radiate an obvious sense of enjoyment, but I hope no one will ever doubt that that is what I have always felt.

From the first moment I played cricket I have played to win. There has never seemed any sense in not doing so. It's a contest and in every contest the principal objective must be to win. But that doesn't mean you can't enjoy a game as it develops, or that you shouldn't be disappointed if the result goes the wrong way. Wilfred Rhodes is supposed to have said, 'We don't play this game for fun', and if he did, I am with the great man all the way. I have never played cricket for fun, but I *have* always played it for pleasure. Perhaps because I am undemonstrative, very few people will ever know just how much pleasure.

Thus it was to be sport which held the key to my future. I must have been a fairly strong character, even at eleven, because I really put my foot down on the matter of going to grammar school. I did not think that perhaps the facilities and the coaching might be better there; I was happy with what I had got and felt it was enough for me to develop what ability I had. It's difficult to say whether at that stage I was thinking in terms of a full-time career in sport. How do you decide what your life is going to be like when you are eleven years old? All I knew was that I didn't want anything to interfere with my way of life at that time.

My best subjects at school were maths and what we called 'workshop drawing' – draughtsmanship, I suppose. I was always reasonably good at practical things like woodwork but I looked on these simply as things you had to do at school; no more than that. You obviously had to do something while you were there, but it didn't seem to me any kind of means to an end. I was in no way unhappy about being at school, but none of my work seemed to have a particular relevance to anything which I saw as really important. Sport was my life. I watched every game Pudsey St Lawrence played, cycling to the away games every other week, so that by the time I went into the Bradford League myself I knew all the grounds.

Girls? Well, there were always one or two young girls around. I was playing for Farsley Second Eleven at fourteen and I was in the first team when I was fifteen, so there were always a few girls looking on admiringly, I suppose. A seat in the back row of the pictures was about ninepence, I think, and a visit there once a week fulfilled the social obligations of taking the girlfriend out. I started going with Shirley when I was thirteen, and though we broke off the affair once or twice she got me in the end! The first break-up occurred when I was fourteen; she went to the grammar school and I left school to start work. The split came because our lives were taking different courses, not as a matter of social or educational snobbery. She came from 't'top end o't'village' in any case, so the social distinction was there to begin with!

Living in Farsley, or Pudsey, we were sandwiched between the cities of Leeds and Bradford, with half a million and three hundred thousand people respectively. Consequently, Leeds was the big city and Bradford was the town to which we naturally gravitated. Also, it was fractionally closer. But I went to the city as little as possible because I was a terrible traveller. I remember once coming back from a day in Leeds with my parents and we all had to get off the bus at Bramley Town End and walk two miles home because I was literally green with travel-sickness. The best form of transport for me was the old bone-shaker tram. The front of the top deck was open, and by sitting there and getting the fresh air I could just about manage the trip into Bradford. In mid-winter it was a toss-up between being sick and suffering from exposure! For holidays we usually went to Bridlington, although that was largely when I was younger. In my early teens we were involved in the war and everyone was encouraged to take holidays at home, but before that the summer holiday used to give me a certain sense of adventure. To travel something like seventy miles was really an event, because you've got to remember that the rest of my life was spent in the atmosphere of a village community. Both Pudsey and Farsley may have Leeds on one side and Bradford on the other, but we belonged to our village and those sprawling places on either side really had nothing to do with us.

So for one week every August it was off to Mrs Tate's lodging-house in Bridlington, the dodg'ems in the fun-fair, days on the beach, long walks up to Flamborough Head and sometimes almost to Filey. I remember Bridlington as a town of bright lights and noise and people we had met in previous years. The tradition of the summer seaside holiday was a strong one, and West Riding people have never lightly broken with tradition. I know families who have gone to the same 'digs' in the same town for as long as thirty years. Being on holiday was something different, but it is not a part of my life I recall as being especially exciting. I even found the North Sea a bit too cold to spend much time in it.

Although my father was self-employed he was never going to be rich. I don't think he made any more than the average working man, so there was never any question of our having our own family car. I never even thought of that as a possibility. But I remember that we always kept a good table and that I was always decently dressed. I hadn't six or seven suits or anything like that, but I looked presentable when necessary, and I was always dressed warmly enough when the weather required it. We didn't need much pocket money because we made our own fun. Just a few 'props' were required to play our sports, and just a little imagination to play our other games. That is what I have never really been able to understand about modern kids. They have ten times as many material things as we had and very much more money in their pockets, yet they are always complaining about being bored. I just don't understand it. My childhood was happy and comfortable and secure and I did not feel the need to ask for anything more than I had. At the pictures our imaginations were fed on the swashbuckling exploits of Errol Flynn and Tyrone Power, and then we went home and translated them into our own terms. All that was needed was a little imagination for the recreation ground to become the Spanish Main, and the boundary wall, the deck of a privateer. We moved into our own world and lived our private fantasies. They were simple and harmless, giving us hours of pleasure and causing no one any disquiet or offence.

The special event of the winter was a visit to the pantomime in Bradford with the chorus of Francis Laidler's Little Sunbeams and the magic of Kirby's Flying Ballet. If our eyes detected the harness and wires which kept the fairies airborne our minds immediately rejected the evidence because that would have spoiled the pleasure. The war, which began when I was seven years old, put out the lights but otherwise I can't remember it making any great impact on my life. Two cousins were involved, one in the army and one in the RAF, and fortunately they both came through without serious injury. My father had to pack up his cabinet-making business and go into munitions. I remember him dropping a shell on his foot in an armaments factory at Rodley and having to have the boot cut away from a broken toe – that sort of thing sticks in the mind, of course; and I can remember the air-raid sirens sounding several times (once only a day or two after war broke out). In fact the sirens were located at the police station, which was only about thirty yards from my home, so it was difficult not to remember them – they certainly made the windows rattle. I remember things like food shortages, and having my first banana after the war. But in general it didn't touch me except in one way: the grass was allowed to grow in the places where I wanted to play games, and we found it a bit difficult to organise a game of cricket on grass a foot long!

*   *   *   *   *

My early school reports at Frances Street Junior Mixed record that at Recitations, Compositions, Language, Literature, General Intelligence, History, Art and Nature Study I was assessed as 'good'. At Reading, Mental Arithmetic and Geography, I was 'very good'. But at Spelling, Written Arithmetic and Scripture, I was classed only as 'fairly good' which was, I think, a kindly euphemism. By the time my final year came round (now at Wesley Street) I was second in a class of twenty and my report ended with a 'special mention' from the headmaster, Mr Ingham: 'He has given great help at cricket. His work in connection with National Savings has been careful and accurate.'

I have no doubt that will bring a smile to the lips of many who have known me through my adult years, because my character was clearly developing as a fourteen-year-old schoolboy. I was keen to be involved, completely involved, in my cricket, and I had learned that it was important to watch the pennies!

Perhaps my mother was slightly more concerned for me to go on to further education than my father was. Mothers tend to think in more ambitious terms, at least as far as a wider scope of learning is concerned. These things were never put into words any more than my half-formed thoughts of a sporting life were given formal expression. While I was shy, even nervous, in company which was not really familiar to me, I had pretty fixed ideas of what my priorities were. At fourteen I didn't sit down and work out what shape my later life was going to take; it was enough for me that my present was happy and secure and that life was pleasant. But I suppose I was developing the idea that if I could continue to enjoy my sport and be able to make a living by doing so, I would have achieved the ideal existence.

Even now, looking back over the thirty-four years since, I find it difficult to see my life taking any other course. There was a sort of inevitability about it all the way through. If I had not been a sportsman, then I suppose I would have become a draughtsman because that was the sort of work I liked best at school and no doubt I would have been content with that. When I was fourteen, simply to be able to take up a job one enjoyed doing was a luxury that not many of my contemporaries enjoyed. Remember that I was a child of the 1930s, and in my world if you had a job (or if your father had a job) at all you were one of the lucky ones.

Because he had had to give up his own business during the war, my father had considerable difficulties in re-establishing a self-employing business afterwards. Fortunately he was a versatile craftsman, qualified as an upholsterer, as a French polisher and as a cabinet-maker. He did joinering and undertaking as well, so he could turn his hand to most things, but it was still a difficult trade because there was an acute shortage of timber for several years after the war. So when I left school and became apprenticed to him in the business it was partly because it seemed a logical thing to do, partly to help him through a difficult time, and partly because there was no problem about time off to play cricket which was already beginning to develop at the Farsley Club. The timber shortage was so acute that at one stage we bought an aeroplane wing to strip down for plywood. It must have been a Mosquito because I remember how well it was glued together and we got very few clean lengths out of it; I had some idea then as to why Mosquito crews had thought so much of their planes!

Difficult though life was for my father at that time, he never created any problem about my taking time off to play for Farsley. Perhaps he sensed before I did that my career might lie in full-time sport, I don't know. It was something we never sat down and talked about formally. In the same way, when I was first picked for Yorkshire, and then England, there were no ecstatic expressions of rejoicing. Just as I think I have never been, my parents were not extravagantly demonstrative. They were pleased and they were proud and they didn't have to put it into so many words. I knew, and we all understood each other.

2
GOLDEN DAYS...

Of our boyhood circle (about fifteen of us) my closest friends were Donald Jones and Eric Hargate, both of whom went to the York-shire nets, too. Donald also went on the Yorkshire Federation tour in which we played for the first time with D. B. Close and F. S. Trueman, who were to play major parts in my adult life. Donald was, I think, probably more gifted as both a cricketer and a footballer than anyone in the village and he was also the fastest runner. I have often found myself reflecting sadly that so much talent was really wasted. He carried on playing League cricket for some years but he drifted away from football and he could have been so good at both sports. It would, I suppose, be im-pertinent of me to complain that his enthusiasm for sport seemed to wane after his marriage – different people look at these things in different ways. Shirley and I have known each other since we were eleven and thirteen respectively, and my sporting life has been hers; not all wives look upon their husband's sporting activities with the same degree of equanimity! Donald Jones and I lived within a few yards of each other in Farsley and we were both sport-mad. We went everywhere together, played our games together, and even shared our seaside summer holidays. When you are young it is difficult to envisage anything changing, especially things to which you are passionately devoted. If I stopped to think about it I visualised Donald and I growing up and becoming better and better at our games, playing for Yorkshire together, for England. Juvenile ambition sets itself no boundaries.

In my mid-teens I was friendly with a boy called Billy Hudson, who introduced me first to billiards and later to golf. Billy was another richly gifted games player. He could make two hundred breaks at billiards and he became a two-handicap golfer. My first club was Fulneck, but later I joined Woodhall Hills, both virtually on our doorstep. I have been a member at Woodhall now for more than twenty years. There I am just another club member who happens to play cricket for a living, rather than being a joiner or a publican or a mill-owner. Inevitably, because the club is in Yorkshire, there is a certain amount of talk about cricket and if a widely-publicised event is taking place I can expect to be asked a question or two. But not aggressively, not inquisitorially. I can relax at my golf club and be one of the members, and I am grateful for that.

I still see all these friends of my youth from time to time and I am always glad to do so, not so much with regret that we drifted apart because one comes to realise the inevitability of this as lives develop on different lines, but with real delight because such meetings take one back to carefree days and events which were of major importance at the time. When you are nine or ten a day out or a cricket match which goes wrong seems like a major disaster; at sixteen or seventeen a broken date can seem like the end of the world. Conversely, the golden days of childhood are hallowed memories and all those associated with them remain important figures in one's life. Donald Jones and Eric Hargate and Billy Hudson were part of growing up, to me; they are part of my life, a part which I remember with warmth and affection.

I remember, too, the anonymous figure of an umpire for Wyther Park School in Leeds. They were the champions of their division and Wesley Street School were champions of our own division so a challenge was issued. I was bowling my seamers, as usual, and threw in a slower ball with a bit of off-spin applied. It turned quite a bit on what was, for schoolboys, a good wicket and the umpire said: 'If you can bowl off-breaks like that, lad, don't waste your time on seamers.' I became captain of the school side and averaged 100 with the bat and my wickets cost two runs each, but it was as a *batsman* all-rounder that I was called up by Yorkshire Colts. If that sounds a bit Irish, I was in the side about sixty or seventy per cent as a batsman with my bowling as a bonus. I was still bowling mainly seamers, turning to spin only occasionally. One of the decisive events in my change to full-time spinning came when I was sixteen or seventeen, playing for Farsley at Saltaire. Jack Firth, that genial character who later became wicket-keeper for Leicestershire, was the man responsible. We had been bowled out for 58 on a rain-affected wicket and our slow left-armer (who was one of the champion non-spinners of all time) was completely ineffective. I was still a painfully shy youngster in those days and it would no more have occurred to me to ask to bowl than it would to turn out for cricket in a kilt. But Jack, who had seen me bowling spinners in the nets, ostentatiously called across to me: 'You can bowl better spinners than this. Get yourself on and give it a go.'

The captain took the hint, I took five for five and Farsley won by three runs. Another step had been taken along the road to a change of trade. However, I was not yet determined on a full-time career in cricket. Certainly I knew that it was going to play a very important part in my life, but in my mid-teens I was equally keen on football and I had a fair amount of ability. I was a wing-half, a position I liked because one was always in the game, either defending or attacking – an all-rounder of soccer, I suppose. I played a certain amount of football at centre-half but strictly speaking I was not as keen on that position as I was on being a wing-half. After leaving school I was with Farsley Celtic for a bit but most of the time, up to eighteen, I played with Pudsey Athletic. They were a good side, consistently doing well in junior football in Leeds. *The* side in the area were Ashley Road, because they were the Leeds United junior side, but we were about on a par with them; it was good football and I thoroughly enjoyed it. Offers came to go for trials with professional clubs – Aston Villa, Huddersfield Town and Bradford City – and it was touch and go, when I was seventeen, between settling on football or cricket as my professional life. In fact I was talked out of taking trials by a member of our football club committee! That probably sounds a bit strange, but Norman Jackson was also a cricketer, with Pudsey St Lawrence. He had seen me playing with Farsley and his advice was: 'Stick to cricket and forget about the football.' This was reinforced by my father who, not without a degree of cynicism, suggested that I would probably break a leg and ruin myself for a career in both games. But football has remained one of my great loves and I have many friends in the game which I watch regularly.

Our team at Pudsey Athletic broke up because most of the boys went for their National Service together, and for the next two years my sporting life was as a member of the Royal Air Force – but not a particularly distinguished member. I could not rid myself of the feeling that it was all a waste of time now that I had decided on a full-time career in cricket and, with all the impatience of an eighteen-year-old, I was anxious to get started properly. Looking at my ability realistically rather than (I trust) immodestly, I was confident I could make the grade. I was shy, particularly in unfamiliar company, but I had a pretty strong character and I could make an honest self-appraisal which assured me that I could do it. Cricket was to be my life; I wanted to get on with it.

Nevertheless, the two years in uniform had to be served so it was a matter of how to make the best of them. I had a stroke of luck there. At my initial square-bashing unit, near Cheltenham, the Postings Officer came from Dishforth, the big airfield beside the A1 about twenty miles north of Leeds, and even at long range he was keen to help the sports record of the station. He told me not to apply for a specific trade, which would send me on a course to any one of half a dozen different places, but to stick rigidly to 'general duties'. This gave him the chance to post me to Dishforth where my first job was as a batman – not exactly the profession I had in mind! However, fairly quickly I was moved to the sports stores and that was much more like it. I played cricket and football for the station and my cricket brought me a place in the Royal Air Force side and Combined Services. In between, by a slightly unauthorised use of the 'night school bus' I was able to enjoy an intermittent social life with Shirley. The bus was laid on to take further education enthusiasts from Dishforth to Leeds and while my academic aspirations were not, perhaps, as idealistic as those of my fellow-passengers, the transport was very handy for a twice-a-week trip to the pictures with my girlfriend.

Service cricket was not the same as county championship, by any means, but it was good fun and the next best way of grooming myself for my post-service career. Cricket was a better paid job than football, and if I had any regrets about abandoning a League soccer career that fact provided a certain amount of consolation. Also the prestige of being a Yorkshire cricketer in the early fifties was no small thing. In the RAF team I roomed with Jim Parks; Freddie Titmus was in the side and Freddie Trueman came in towards the tail end of my service because his two years in uniform had been deferred. I played under two captains; Bob Wilson and Alan Shirreff. Shirreff, despite a rather extensive career which took him to Cambridge University, Kent, Hampshire and Somerset, was the only one who behaved like an officer first and a cricketer second and we put him right within a couple of games! Perhaps his view of us was coloured a little by an occasion when a bloke in mufti, a stranger to us all, wandered into the dressing-room and not unnaturally was regarded by us all with total indifference. As he turned out to be an Air Marshal, our leader, Squadron Leader Shirreff, was a little put out at the lack of respect shown by his flock.

In one game against the Army at Lord's I came up against D. B. Close, with whose life and career mine has been interwoven since our boyhood. In all my first-class career I never bagged a pair but on a steamy, swingy morning in this two-day game at Lord's I got 0 and 0. Closey did me in the first innings and caught me in the second – the only pair I have to my name in all my cricket.

3
LEAGUE PLAYER
OF PROMISE

My friend Donald Jones got into Farsley's first team before I did, though neither of us had reached the age of sixteen when the call came. Donald and I had been inseparable companions for years, as I have said, completely united in our love of cricket, and yet our temperaments were entirely different, at least as far as the game was concerned. Perhaps the most extreme emotion I have experienced throughout my career has been determination. If I have felt apprehension or delight or anger or disappointment it has been a matter of the utmost importance to me not to show it. This has not been a conscious thing – simply a straightforward manifestation of my character. I am not, and never have been, demonstrative. I am not going to say, as journalists have written occasionally, that the tougher a situation, the more I enjoy it. If you sit down coldly and consider the implications of those words it is self-evident that they make nonsense. What would be more correct to say is that the tougher a situation, the more determined I become to cope with it.

Donald, by contrast, was highly-strung in the extreme and it was not uncommon for him to be literally sick while waiting to go in to bat. I know first-class players today – good players – who experience the same problem. He got into the Farsley first team during the 1947 season and after getting runs initially, he then had a couple of failures and asked to be put back into the second team. I got my chance and ironically it was against Pudsey St Lawrence, the club I might have been with but for that family move 'up the village'. We just scraped home in a low-scoring match, and as I remember it I got 20-odd not out and three for 14. At the end of the match our captain (Harry Bailes, a great Bradford League character) said: 'Now for crying out loud, don't *you* go and ask to go back to the second team.' My reaction was immediate and spontaneous: 'Don't worry. There's no way I'm going to want to go back.' I stayed in Farsley's first team after that.

I was in Pudsey St Lawrence's third team when I was eleven, in Farsley's Second Eleven at thirteen and at fifteen I was now established as a Bradford League first-teamer. I was a few days short of my seventeenth birthday when Farsley met Pudsey in a Priestley Cup match.

The Priestley Cup is (and has been since 1904) the knock-out competition of the League and in 1949 it was played to a finish on a timeless basis. When one side reached 150 its innings was suspended and the other side went in. If *they* reached 150, they then gave way to the first team, and so it went on until a side was bowled out. So a match which started on a Saturday could continue through every evening of the following week, especially as there was a lot of batting strength around at the time. That particular game against Pudsey started when I was sixteen years old and I was seventeen by the time it had finished! I had also scored 148 runs. Although we were beaten in the final by Yeadon (from whom Brian Close graduated that season to Yorkshire), my score was the highest in the Cup competition of 1949 which put me in some rather distinguished company.

In fact even a cursory glance at the records shows just how much the Bradford League has given to first-class cricket over the years. In 1933 Len Hutton was the highest Priestley Cup scorer with 108. In 1941 it was my future team-mate and captain, Vic Wilson, followed in 1942 by Sid Buller, who was to become a great umpire after a professional career with Worcestershire. In 1954, Doug Padgett scored 124 not out, while two years later Bryan Stott (another member of the side who were to bring the County Championship back to Yorkshire in 1959) was the top Cup scorer with 133 not out. Other players who are in that list of records are Eric Barraclough and Bernard Brooke, who both played for Yorkshire; Lewis Pickles, who went to Somerset; Duncan Fearnley (to Worcestershire); Harry Cartwright (to Derbyshire); Tony Clarkson (to Somerset) and Neil Smith (to Essex). In between, the war years saw the importation of George Pope (from Derbyshire), Les Berry (from Leicestershire), Walter

Keeton (from Nottinghamshire) and Eddie Paynter (from Lancashire). If you go back to World War I you can find the names of John Berry Hobbs (132 in 1917) and the immortal S. F. Barnes (168 in 1918): and Barnes did the hat-trick in the final that year! The Bradford League is proud of its illustrious history and the names it has given to cricket – and rightly so. It was the sternest of testing-grounds for a teenager learning his trade in those years after the war when crowds flocked to watch sport of all kinds.

That marathon tie with Pudsey went on right through the week, with our final score reaching 394 and we won by about 100 runs. I remember it as a week of beautiful weather – in fact I think I had a touch of sunstroke. Spectators who arrived at the ground later than half-past five couldn't get in, so that meant there were two or three thousand watching in a marvellous atmosphere of fierce partisanship. I was a slight, almost frail, teenager, and outside the cricketing context a not very mature sixteen-year-old when I went into that match; I sometimes wonder just how much that innings in that atmosphere did for me. With no restriction on the number of overs it was a perfect situation for a youngster trying to develop his own game, and I have been saddened by the disappearance of that form of cricket from the Bradford League. Now, as Yorkshire's manager, I regard it as a matter of urgency to try to persuade the League to restore a form of cricket which enables young players to learn how to build a big innings and which encourages bowlers (and captains) to attack rather than contain.

I was nineteen when I beat my own best score of 148 with one of 162 not out in Farsley's opening game of the 1952 season. We were put in by Saltaire and totalled 253 for three and, without knowing it, I probably missed a League record. Since 1919 the record for the highest individual total in any game has been recorded as 'W. Payton, Bankfoot v Great Horton, 187 not out'. I had a fairly slow start against Saltaire and took eighty-six minutes to reach 50, but I was 100 only twenty-two minutes later and another twenty-two minutes after that I was 150 with seven sixes and seventeen fours. By then I had been joined by my friend Donald Jones. He had settled in well and I thought, 'There's a 50 on for him here if he can get enough of the strike'. A score of 50 meant a collection. So I pushed for one for the next half hour until Donald got his 50, and when he was out one run later we declared. It was only afterwards that I learned about the record which must have been 'on' because I was going well and there was time to spare. Would I have played differently if I had known? I've often wondered about that myself, but I'm still glad I helped a pal get a 50, and a collection. After all, 162 not out wasn't a bad score to have against my name. I don't regard records as the be-all and end-all of a career, but at the same time I don't despise them either. They are a part of the history and the folk-lore of any game; they provide talking-points and anything that starts, and keeps, people talking about a sport is a good thing. I enjoy looking back on such events because they conjure up memories which are important to me and which give me a great deal of pleasure.

In later years Yorkshire's formidable personal press corps were always keeping an eye on statistical milestones, led by that re-doubtable pair, John Bapty of the *Yorkshire Evening Post* and Dick Williamson, of the *Bradford Telegraph and Argus*. Thus, when I celebrated my Yorkshire cap in 1955 with a century against the MCC at Scarborough, I learned that it was the thousandth century scored for the county. When I played for England for the first time – against New Zealand at Old Trafford in 1958 – I read that I was the fiftieth Yorkshireman to play for his country. Cricket is very much a game of facts and records and statistics, and I am certainly not unhappy to have a place amongst them.

But all that was in the future. My present was that of a League player of promise who had been invited to the Yorkshire nets. The door to my future was opening. To look at my batting at Headingley there was Arthur Mitchell – tough, uncompromising 'Ticker', with no honeyed polish to temper his critiques. Arthur's messages may have come from the heart but they had the appearance (or rather the sound) of having come straight from the shoulder. He had no time for those who were not willing to give a hundred and one per cent of their time to learn. My bowling came under the gentler – but no less honest – appraisal of Bill Bowes. And watching all with a fatherly eye was the cherubic figure of Maurice Leyland, a pre-war player no less loved by his fellow professionals than he was by his countless admirers who watched cricket the world over. My fellow students included one F. S. Trueman, but a Trueman unrecognisable when you think of his comfortable, expensively-suited, cigar-smoking presence of the 1980s. How could anyone have believed that thirty years on this thin, pasty-faced, narrow-chested waif, with unruly, unkempt hair falling over his right eye and ear, would be radio's sporting personality of the year, and a star of television in a variety of roles in continents twelve thousand miles apart? Who, indeed, could have believed that over the next twenty years he was to be one of the great fast bowlers of all time? There was Brian Close ... massive, indestructible, built (it seemed, then as now) of steel and concrete and endowed with all the talent in the world as a games-player. There were others, who flickered more briefly across the screen of Yorkshire's future, but with these two, F.S. and Closey, the next thirty years of my life were to be closely interwoven.

In 1950 I had played regularly for Yorkshire's Colts; in 1951 my first-team chance came. But caps bearing a white rose were not distributed lightly at that time; I had a long apprenticeship to serve before I had one of those.

4
MY BRIDE - AND MY BEST MAN

At fifteen I could have appeared on a television quiz programme and answered any question put to me on sporting records (except that my basic shyness would have prevented my getting up there before an audience in the first place). Simply in terms of knowing my stuff I could certainly have done it, because my boyhood reading was almost exclusively in this field. I didn't read any of the recognised 'boys' books' but I had an insatiable appetite for sporting literature of any kind. I devoured it, memorising records and facts and statistics and career highlights. But I absolutely could not have got up before an audience for any reason at all. Even today I couldn't, for instance, get up and sing a song, no matter how light-hearted and friendly the occasion. I used to watch Philip Sharpe and Don Wilson go through their Black and White Minstrels routines in the sixties in pubs, clubs, and hotel lounges – they didn't need any encouragement; they'd sing with or without an audience for the sheer joy of it. I could never do anything like that. It wasn't until the tail-end of my last Australian tour, when I had made hundreds of speeches, that I overcame the feeling of being uncomfortable at speaking in public. Yet I am not a loner. On the contrary, I think I would go crackers if I had to live by myself. I have always enjoyed being with my family. After the strain of five days of Test cricket – and it can *be* a strain – what I liked to do best, if there was a free day, was to go back home and Shirley and I would take the girls up on to Ilkley Moor with a picnic. We'd find a spot by a stream, put a couple of cans of beer in to cool and sit and listen to the radio. That was the ideal form of relaxation for me. I like to be with my own people. It is, perhaps, an attitude born of my childhood. I was an only child and we were therefore a small but happy family unit. Shirley and

I have two daughters, so our family unit is not much bigger, and we are close to each other, involved with each other and we have a good family life. My childhood holidays were spent in Bridlington; our children go to Spain with us – nothing elaborate, just a simple relaxation in the sun.

Bright lights and a big social scene have never attracted me and I don't believe in wasting money in frivolous ways. I am happy to pay for a nice house and a good car but I wouldn't dream of gambling.

I love to play bridge, and I play it to win no matter how modest the stakes. I like my game of golf and I'll always have a side bet on that. But in both those contexts I am betting on my own ability to win and that seems straightforward enough to me. It is a matter of skill. I certainly wouldn't play for ridiculous stakes or indulge in a wild gamble when I had no personal control over the outcome. When you have been brought up in a normal working-class home you learn to appreciate the value of money a good deal better than many people today. If my father had a couple of weeks with no work coming into the cabinet-making business (and I can remember that occurring) there was no question of hopping down to the social security and living off someone else. When that happened, we did without things until the work did come in. I have never forgotten those days and inevitably they have influenced my view of things and the way I have run my own life.

Shirley and I had known each other for thirteen years when we were married at Farsley Parish Church in 1958. We went to Blackpool for our honeymoon, staying at the Imperial Hotel. I put out my brand new shoes that night to be cleaned and never saw them again! Vicky was born in 1961 and Diane in 1965. In the early part of our marriage I felt I would like a son so that I could watch him develop as a sportsman. Then I thought: 'Suppose he is not a sportsman – how would I feel then?' Most of all we wanted children who were healthy and happy, and we have no complaints at all. Anyway, girls think more of their fathers, don't they?

My best man was Brian Close, whom I had known since we were boys at the Yorkshire nets. He then lived in Rawdon, which was only about five miles away from Farsley, but he played in the Airedale and Wharfedale League which meant his cricket world was a different one from mine, in the Bradford League. In any case, five miles seems half the earth away when you are a no-car family. However, we roomed together in my early days with Yorkshire until Closey developed an interest in wrestling which he found necessary to practise on me at rather unsocial hours. After I had been awakened once or twice at seven a.m. and found myself in a back hammer-lock, he had to go. We also used to drive together between games which means that I am exceedingly fortunate to be alive! Closey's driving has been a legend in first-class cricket for thirty years and men with the strongest of nerves have aged visibly in the course of one journey as his passenger. I found it infinitely harder to sit beside him as we drove from one game to the next than to do the driving myself.

It became a matter of habit to warn him, the voice rising in shrill hysteria, that the driver in front was braking as Closey's attention wandered. And sure enough, nine times out of ten we would go sliding into the back of the preceding car. Mercifully, I was not in any of the five cars he has written off in his career but I've had my share of adventures. When he had a Humber Hawk we were driving out of Manchester and he spotted another Hawk coming up behind. His reaction was immediate, and quite, quite predictable: 'This so-and-so is not going to pass me.' It was only when the bells started ringing that we knew it was a police car! Closey always had to be the first to arrive at the town where we were playing next, even if he left the previous ground after everybody else. As he passed each car in turn – because at the speeds he drove he was always going to pass everyone – he would cackle delightedly and give them a wave. As sure as fate, the others would then overtake *him* a couple of miles down the road as he was giving his particulars to the police! On one occasion he gave the V-sign to Tony Nicholson and Bob Platt, the last car to be overtaken on one particular lunatic chase and in doing so he omitted to notice a diversion sign. Fearing the worst, Tony and Bob gently followed down the road from which traffic had been diverted and found the car upside down in a hole, the wheels still spinning, and a white-faced P. J. Sharpe (Closey's passenger) climbing out of the roadworks. Closey? Indestructible as ever, he was standing at the side of the hole, calling down the wrath of the gods upon the idiot who had dug up the road without telling

29

him personally! He once smashed up two new cars in a day. Coming into York one afternoon on his way back from Scarborough, he took a bend in the road that was no longer there and landed in the middle of a rather startled picnic party. It's never his fault, of course. He once drove into and overturned a three-ton truck – but he was, he said, only doing thirty miles an hour! Thirty miles an hour? Closey has never got down to thirty, even from a standing start . . .

He didn't slow down as he got older, either. Shortly after arriving at Somerset he was driving along a country lane and listening with his usual avid interest to the racing results on a transistor radio. As he took a corner, the radio slid across the car and he reached across to retrieve it. The result of the 2.30 at Sandown Park was, of course, far more important than any instincts of self-preservation. The car ploughed into a thick, thorn hedge, mowing it down until the car lost momentum and came to a halt, astride what was left of the hedge. As Closey sat there, cursing the fools who put hedges beside roads and made transistors which slid across cars, a farmer drove his tractor round the corner and stopped in some bewilderment. He addressed the fuming county captain thus in the ripe accents of the Quantocks: 'That be a danged funny place to park 'ee car.'

Everyone who has ever had any dealings with D. B. Close has a love-hate relationship with him. No, 'hate' is too strong a word . . . a love-exasperation relationship. If he is your friend, he is a staunch and a loyal friend. He is godfather to my elder daughter, Vicky, and he never fails to arrive to see her on Christmas Eve. We all know his faults but I can't think of anyone who doesn't forgive him for them. He has driven all his friends mad at one time or another but somehow no one lets it rankle for very long. He and I made a good team as captain of Yorkshire and senior player perhaps because of different characters and temperaments. Concentration is not Brian's strong suit, especially when not much is happening. When he was attacking there was no better cricket captain anywhere, but perhaps if we were fielding on a good wicket his attention would wander. That was when I could say to him, 'Come on, Closey, let's try this, or that'. And he would always take my advice. When I had to tell him to get stuffed on occasions (as, on occasions, I did) he would take it from me when he wouldn't have taken it from anyone else. I think we have always had a basic respect for each other in every way, and I was very happy to serve under him in the Yorkshire team of the sixties. It never occurred to me to wish I was the skipper. It was a good side; it was a happy side; it was a winning side; it was a well-led side and I was part of that leadership. I was quite content with that. When, later, we found ourselves as opposing captains of different counties we had some tremendous duels, each trying to out-think the other.

I remember one Gillette Cup tie between Somerset and Leicestershire at Taunton which, threequarters of the way through the game, we had virtually lost. There seemed simply nothing we could do about it when things started to go wrong for Somerset. Every captain knows what that is like, because they have all experienced it at one time or another. A catch went down; a four was edged; and then Jim Parks, the wicket-keeper, had to go off with a bruised thumb. Closey took over behind the stumps and as we crept closer to their total he took off the pads to give himself a bit more mobility. When it got to the last ball he took off the gloves as well – and Alan Jones bowled four wides down the leg side! Closey took off like an Olympic diver and landed with an earth-shattering crash about two yards wide of the leg stump, but he couldn't reach the ball. We had won the tie and my old friend lay beating his fists on the ground and moaning to himself, 'How can you skipper a side with idiots like that in it?' A couple of years later, Norman McVicker hit two sixes off the last two balls of a John Player League game to win that match for Leicestershire – and if you haven't guessed the name of the bowler, it was Alan Jones. He moved on to Middlesex to play quite a part in their county championship success in 1976 but I think he was a bit of a trial to Closey on one or two occasions.

I mentioned the matter of concentration a little earlier. Brian was the senior off-spinner in the early fifties and I remember playing against Gloucester at Bristol with Len Hutton skippering the side. Tom Graveney came in and Len took off Brian and gave me the ball saying: 'I want you to bowl four or five maiden overs at this chap. That's all I want you to do – just make him work.' So I bowled at Tom, a fine player, giving him absolutely nothing, and in fact I got him out. Len said, 'Thank you very much. Right, now you take over, Brian'. I think I was rather aggrieved at the time at being taken off. It was only later I really appreciated the full significance of what we had done and I had learned one more lesson about knowing opposition weaknesses and thinking them out. I concentrated harder on my bowling than Brian, who relied on natural gifts. He could bowl superbly but he bowled more bad balls than I did. I learned very early in my career that batsmen are rather selfish people, and I have never really believed in 'buying' wickets. It doesn't often come off and I have never been very keen on suddenly finding my analysis at none for 70 off seven. That happened to me once at Scarborough ... Festival cricket ... with Godfrey Evans and Frank Tyson batting.

They said, 'Throw us a few up to hit, then we'll get out'. I did, but they didn't, and I never fell for that particular con trick again. Being an all-rounder has a lot of advantages, one of which is that you can read a bowler's mind – and a batsman's. Or at least you can try to work out how they are thinking. I once got 80 out of a total of just over 200 against Kent with big Norman Graham bowling on a wicket that was seaming, and I played as well as I have ever done in my life. Norman, six feet and seven inches of him, was not the easiest of blokes to smash around at the best of times and here he was bowling with his head on a helpful wicket. But somehow I read what he was going to do and it worked out right, every time. If he bowled one short I was waiting for it. If it was up to me I was on the front foot waiting for it, and I know I played really well. That evening, over a drink, Norman asked: 'I'm damn sure you knew what I was going to bowl today before the ball came, didn't you?'

Sometimes, of course, you don't get it right, as on one occasion very early in my career when Brian Statham bowled me a bouncer. I was quite sure he wouldn't bowl another and I was wrong. Two in two was very rare from 'George', and the second one I sent straight up in the air. I learned something that day. In fact you learn something in practically every day's cricket you play.

5
MY BRIDEGROOM-
SHIRLEY'S STORY

My first boyfriend was small, diffident and so unbelievably shy that people who have known him only in adult life could never have credited it. We were together at Wesley Street School and although there was three years difference in our ages – a yawning gap when you are children – it was nevertheless established that I was Raymond Illingworth's girlfriend. It was not a blazing romance which made a dramatic impact on our young world; it was just an understanding amongst our circle that I was his girl and he was my boy. And then, as these things happen when you are young, we simply drifted apart with a kind of inevitability over which we had no control. Raymond left school at fourteen to start work, I went on to grammar school about the same time, and our worlds were suddenly a long way apart. It has always been Raymond's family joke that because I went to grammar school while he joined the ranks of the working class I had suddenly become too posh for him to be my escort any more. And as I lived at one end of Farsley (the end he described as the 'top-enders') and Raymond at the other, the gulf automatically became wider. But it *was* a joke. We were geographically and educationally separated, not socially.

I didn't see him in anything other than the casual sense – in the distance, really – for something like six years, but something must have lingered on from the Wesley Street days because when a friend of his, John Percival, rang up to ask if I would go out with Raymond, I agreed. Obviously he was still as shy as ever! Somehow I imagined he would be the same in every other way, which meant he would be small and slight. In the meantime I had grown into a young woman of seventeen and there was only one thing to do to avoid embarrassing Raymond – I put on my flat heels so I didn't tower over him. So it came as quite a surprise to me to find that he had grown up, too, and now he was quite a bit taller than me.

We spent our first date at Pudsey Feast. That is the annual West Riding town holiday when mills close and most people in those days went off to Scarborough or Bridlington, Blackpool or Morecambe. No one had ever heard of the Costa Brava or Majorca, let alone thought about taking a holiday there. For those who stayed at home there was the Feast fairground and band concerts and dances. If my romance started at Wesley Street School, it was put on a formal footing at Pudsey Feast, 1952, and it has continued ever since.

For the next six years we were officially 'courting' and the idea that we would eventually get married grew upon us rather than suddenly being mentioned on a romantic, moonlit occasion. What was conventional in novelette terms was far from the accepted pattern of our lives. I can't remember any formal proposal; Raymond simply bought me an engagement ring on my twenty-second birthday. By then there was a definite understanding between us, but in good, practical Yorkshire terms there was no point in buying an engagement ring until we had worked out the details of getting married – buying and furnishing our own home. But as for a formal proposal ... well, I don't think anyone who knows Raymond can really see him getting down on one knee and making his declaration!

At that time I was working in the office of a textile mill where my father was the cashier and my grandfather had been the general manager – a family connection which in its own way was traditional. Raymond was now established in the Yorkshire side and we could at last think about getting married. We bought a house five or six months before the wedding so that we had furnished all the downstairs rooms and one bedroom by the time we were married, on 20 September, 1958. The house was paid for and we had a solid foundation to our life together. The prices seem ridiculous by modern standards – £2,100 for the house, between £300 and £400 for the furniture and fittings. But if that seems to be doing it 'on the cheap', you have to remember that £2,500 in 1958 was an astronomical figure for a young, working-class couple to have got together. We had both worked hard to save it because we both had a built-in loathing of debt, a legacy of our upbringing in fiercely proud West Riding homes where our parents always insisted on being able to hold up their heads as 'owing nowt to nobody'.

I continued to work until the birth of our first daughter, Vicky, three years later, and she was barely a year old when Raymond went on his first tour to Australia. In those days players were away for six and a half months, and for the first four Vicky fretted terribly because she was missing her father. A friend brought over some flowers on Christmas Day which Raymond had arranged, and he brought a little toy for Vicky but she was, of course, too young to understand that this meant her father and his friends were thinking about us. That separation was a bit of an ordeal, the more so because of the effect upon a child who was, after all, only a baby.

On his return to England we went to London Airport to meet him and Vicky, now toddling, went straight to him as he came out of the customs hall. It was uncanny in a child of eighteen months – she went straight to him. It was just a little less endearing that my reunion with my husband was celebrated by our daughter standing up in her cot all night shouting 'Dada, Dada'!

I have never regretted not having a son and I don't think Raymond has, either. Certainly he has never given any indication of it. He has always been very close to both girls just as both he and I always had close relationships with our own families. Until the children came along my parents used to go out socially with us and we were more like a group of four friends. Consequently, we never had any baby-sitting problems when the girls came along.

Vicky, at eighteen, is very much the smartly-groomed young lady; Diane, who was born four years later, is the tomboy and a natural at every kind of sport. She is a good sprinter and after being a member of the school netball team she decided she would go to a hockey practice and walked straight into the team. She won the high jump and, just for fun, picked up a javelin and threw it further than the girls who were entered for that event. At the age of fourteen she went to the Pudsey St Lawrence cricket ground with the two boys from next door who play there, and at the end of the practice Diane decided to try it out herself in the nets. A man was watching who said he was talent-spotting for Bradford Ladies' cricket team, and would Diane like to go along to one of their practice-sessions? She went and came home to announce, 'I'm playing at Nottingham on Saturday'. She's just a natural and whatever she tries, she does well at it.

It didn't matter to me particularly in 1958 that I was marrying a Yorkshire cricketer; as far as I was concerned I was marrying Raymond, the man I wanted to marry, and the fact that he played for the county side was coincidental. Of course, I was interested in cricket as I think everyone born in Yorkshire is, to a greater or lesser extent. But I had been just as happy watching him play for Farsley who were a good side and I went regularly with my father to see them. And yet I am grateful for the way in which cricket has given me a richer and fuller life and enabled me to see places and meet people that I might never have done, otherwise.

I have been to Australia and to the West Indies. I have had cocktails at Clarence House with Queen Elizabeth the Queen Mother, visited 10 Downing Street at the invitation of two prime ministers – and, politics aside, I think I found it easier to chat to Harold Wilson than to Edward Heath. It was not that Mr Heath was anything less than a charming host, but Sir Harold is, after all, a West Yorkshire man so it was much easier to find common topics. Cricket has been good to me and I am grateful for it, but I think my favourite place of all is a little place in Spain, near Torremolinos, which has been our family holiday home for years. We go back time after time to a place which has so many happy memories for all of us. As a family, as well as individually, we seem to have grown up there.

It would be silly to pretend there haven't been problem times but they have been problems outside the family and we have been able to face them and cope with them together. When Raymond took on the Yorkshire committee over the question of a contract I felt he was absolutely right and the committee unreasonable. No player had a single thing in writing and could, therefore, have no feeling of security. Raymond fought on behalf of *all* Yorkshire's cricketers and now does it all again but from a different standpoint. In 1968 we discussed it together and I typed the letter of resignation on the morning he went in to deliver his ultimatum.

36

Even then it shouldn't have happened and wouldn't have happened if the committee had not been so intractable. Raymond left, that morning, with the letter in his pocket, about ninety-nine per cent determined to resign if the committee continued to be unreasonable. He didn't want to leave Yorkshire but he felt someone had to make a stand. However, he still hoped that someone would be prepared to compromise. Less than two hours after he left home to go to Headingley, the lady next door came round to say, 'Have you heard on the radio? Raymond's resigned'. Obviously it shouldn't have happened as quickly as that but clearly there was no mood of sweet reasonableness at Yorkshire's headquarters at that time.

As things turned out, I never regretted his doing it and going to Leicestershire because we had a super ten years there. We kept on our home in Pudsey because both girls were at school but we could join Raymond at weekends and during school holidays and, in fact, we saw more of him than we had when he was playing for Yorkshire.

It had often been further to come back from Yorkshire's home games in places like Middlesbrough, Scarborough and Hull than it was to return to Leicester from Nottingham, Derby and Northampton. At first we stayed in an hotel, but as eating out became more expensive we rented a house during the season. Moving from one county club to another we had a ready-made set of friends and we made more during our ten years in Leicester – good friends who are still our friends and will remain so. Those ten years Raymond was with Leicestershire were very happy ones for all of us.

I received the news of a possible return by Raymond to Yorkshire CCC with certain misgivings. Remembering what had happened ten years earlier, it was difficult to believe that attitudes had changed so much. As it happened, I found they had, but I must confess my first reaction was one of foreboding. However, we were warmly received back into the fold and Raymond very quickly threw himself into his new job with enthusiasm and a good deal of hope. He has obviously had disappointments in his first season but he is not a man to give up anything easily and I know it will come right in the end. He has always worked hard at whatever job he has taken on and no one could have worked harder, or worried more, than he did in his first season as the Yorkshire manager. Of course, some people expected him to work miracles straight away; of course, there are always people who are too quick to criticise and who can make hurtful and damaging remarks and it is not easy when such remarks are reported to me. You can't really go round shouting a defence of your husband and Raymond would go mad if I even thought about doing that. That is one of the problems of living your life, to a great extent, through someone else. Raymond's life has been my life for well over twenty years now and I wouldn't have had it any other way. It has been a good life ... a very good life.

6

UP AGAINST THE HARD MEN

In 1951 I was a National Serviceman at Dishforth when I was selected to play for Combined Services, along with Brian Close, who was stationed not far away at Catterick, in the army. Before the game, however – in fact only a couple of days after the team was announced – Yorkshire decided to call me up for the game against Hampshire at Headingley because they were depleted by Test calls. John Nash, the Yorkshire secretary, put in a call to the Station Commander at Dishforth, who was Group Captain Nash! They were not related but perhaps the coincidence of having the same name proved useful, because I was allowed to choose which game to play and there was no hesitation on my part, of course. The man who actually put the choice before me was one Squadron Leader Larry Lamb, later to achieve fame as an international rugby referee.

So off I went to Leeds for my first taste of county championship cricket. It was Yorkshire's last home fixture of the season and the three-day game was very much better supported in 1951 than it is today. Even with Len Hutton and Willie Watson out of the side there was massive support, and I had no time to feel nervous about my debut because seventy minutes after the start of the game I was out in the middle, batting for Yorkshire. Vic Cannings – on his day and the right sort of pitch one of the most devastating swing and seam-bowlers in the game – had bowled Harry Halliday for six, Ted Lester for 17, Vic Wilson for seven and Billy Sutcliffe for seven. Yorkshire were 40 for four when I joined Norman Yardley. We were 136 for five when Cannings bowled me and I had made 56 of the stand of 96 with my skipper. Norman was a great help, offering the odd word of encouragement but never overdoing it. Never once did he tell me to hang on as best I could and just stay there; on the contrary, he urged me to play my shots. To this day I can still enjoy the little thrill of pleasure it gave me as at least half a dozen cover drives raced across the turf to the winter shed (where the county offices now stand). Now that might surprise people who saw me bat later in my career, when I used to gather a lot of runs in the mid-wicket and square-leg area – but at nineteen the cover drive was my delight.

This was Norman Yardley at his best ... encouraging a youngster. He was a thoroughly nice man and in some ways his strength in this direction was his weakness in another. The three players of great stature in the side were Len Hutton, Bob Appleyard and Johnny Wardle. One went his own way and gave little or no help to the captain, while the other two were a law unto themselves and did exactly as they wanted. My first taste of the hardness of Bob Appleyard came in that very first game. I was fielding at wide mid-on and Appleyard was hit high over mid wicket. I was late picking it up against a dark background and consequently a bit late setting off and I missed the catch. Well, Appleyard gave me the biggest rollicking I had ever had in my life up to that point, and bigger than anything I was to experience in the future. You can imagine how I felt, standing there being dressed down in my first match with ten thousand people looking on. Appleyard made no attempt to disguise the sort of thing that was being said. Ten thousand people saw me being blasted like a little schoolboy. I saw Appleyard at his toughest in my first game, and in my view his character never changed.

What has to be said for Appleyard is that he was a great bowler and he always wanted to bowl. There have been bowlers of the highest reputation over the years who just didn't want to know if conditions were against them or a batsman was well in and in top form, but Appleyard was never one of those. In fact he went to the other extreme and simply wouldn't come off. There has always been a lot of speculation over the years as to why that team of the 1950s never won anything. It contained just about the best batting line-up in the world and if the bowling was not quite as strong, the attack included three England men in Trueman, Appleyard and Wardle. Yet we never won a championship from 1949 to 1959. In the mid-fifties we might have done so on a couple of occasions by winning a couple of games which slipped away, and I think on both occasions it was because Appleyard simply would not come off. I can recall the captain saying to me, 'Take over at that end next over', and when I walked over Appleyard was peeling off his sweater and preparing to carry on. 'What do you want?' he asked. 'Skipper has told me to bowl', I replied. 'Bugger off. I'm bowling here', said Appleyard, and that was it. Nothing was said to him; and I had to retreat in some embarrassment.

That was the tragedy of Norman Yardley. He was too nice a chap to stand up to the hard men. In those days every youngster in the side used to dread the ball coming to him and one of the men largely responsible for this was Johnny Wardle. In one game Mick Cowan dropped a catch and while he was still in the middle of apologising Wardle interrupted, with icy bitterness, 'It's my own bloody fault for putting you there'. Such was the hard, vicious school in which the young players of the fifties had to make their way. No word of encouragement, no helpful tips, no pat on the back which would have meant so much from these established Test players – and heaven help you if things went wrong. There was no mitigation, no excuse accepted, no allowances made. You either swallowed the insults and gritted your teeth or you went to pieces. As I have said, we all dreaded the ball coming near us. What a difference after 1959 when Ronnie Burnet had changed things. Everyone wanted the ball to come to him. We stood underneath the skier, not quaking at the possible consequences of a miss but rejoicing that an opportunity had come to take a catch which we knew would not be dropped. It was the simple difference between developing ability and destroying it.

Wardle was a hard man in quite a different way from Appleyard. He was a superb bowler and, in some ways, the complete professional. He was always punctual, always immaculately turned out on the field. If you wanted a net during the afternoon when Yorkshire were batting he would always go out and bowl to you; not every Test bowler in the history of the game has been willing to do that! But he had an acid tongue and he could be devastatingly critical of young players, as in the case of Mick Cowan. I had had my share too, but the last straw came in a game at Sheffield when he pitched into me for dropping a catch. I gave him a right mouthful in return and he was rather taken aback. Afterwards he took me on one side and asked why I had rounded on him. 'What did you expect?' I asked him. 'I don't drop catches deliberately. No one does. And you know damn well I'm a pretty good fielder so what's the point of going on like you do if I happen to miss one?' After that we were fine. He positioned me specially in the outfield and I took about thirty catches off Wardle in a season. But first I had to stand up to him.

Now this is where to my mind the captain showed some weakness. Yardley hated trouble and would keep right out of the way if there was any around. That is where Len Hutton could have helped if he had been the sort of great senior professional that I believe Herbert Sutcliffe was to Brian Sellers. But Len never gave helpful advice; if he made any comment at all it was usually in a mickey-taking way. This was so terribly sad because to me he was the greatest player in the world. I had grown up hero-worshipping him, gone miles to watch him bat. If he had felt like giving me advice I would have devoured every word of it. But just once I asked him something and he treated it with contempt in front of a group of pressmen. I felt about two inches tall, but fortunately one of the reporters was John Bapty, who used to write cricket for the *Yorkshire Evening Post* and he was a grand chap. He told me not to take it to heart and explained that that was Len's natural way of talking to anyone. So the greatest batsman was no more use to the captain in communicating with the rest of the team than two of our Test bowlers. Len was a loner. In those days we used to book our own accommodation and it was the usual thing to find one group of players, for a game at Lord's, say, staying together in one hotel, a second group in another – and Len by himself, usually at the Great Western. And so we won nothing all through the fifties with, on paper, a great team of individual players.

I think if Norman Yardley could have captained Yorkshire after Ronnie Burnet had improved things in 1959 he could have been a great success because then the hard men had gone and we had a team all pulling together. And captaincy is so much more than winning the toss and directing operations on the field, no matter how expertly this is done. It's all about knowing your players and how to get the best out of them; knowing when to give someone a rollicking and when to give him a word of encouragement. It's knowing when a player is 'down', and knowing why he's down. It's knowing when to have a friendly pint with a chap and when to leave him strictly alone to work something out himself. It's understanding people and how to deal with them, because everyone is different in one way or another.

After Norman Yardley came Billy Sutcliffe, and I think everyone knows that he had rather a tough deal. Being the son of the great Herbert was an immense burden for anyone playing with Yorkshire. Billy tried very hard to do the right thing and one example of this was in standing up to Johnny Wardle. As an England bowler, and the senior spinner, Wardle was given the choice of ends; occasionally, when I was operating at the other end and managed to turn one or two, he would immediately want to change to that end. After this had happened once or twice, Billy cottoned on and stood firm: 'No, you've picked your end – now bowl at it.' He did everything he could to get things going on the right lines because he knew what was wrong and what was needed to put things right.

Frankly, Johnny Wardle didn't help. He was a magnificent bowler and we all appreciated it, but he was not much of a help to anyone by his attitude. To the crowds he was the lovable joker on the field, the man who would pocket a hot catch at gulley, then turn round and scan the horizon as if the ball had flashed past him to the boundary. It was one of his tricks of the trade and the crowds loved it, as well as his batting. He could be a very entertaining striker of the ball and he had the knack of making it appear from the sidelines that he was laughing and joking with everyone. That was a long, long way from the truth. Perhaps his attitude was a product of his early days when he was struggling for his place in the late 1940s. Yorkshire tried other slow left-armers like Ronnie Wood and Alan Mason, and for a long time it looked as though they were thinking, 'Anyone but Wardle. There *must* be someone else.' Whether it was this that made him a bit bitter once he was established, I don't know, but I think it must have had a lot to do with it.

When Ronnie Burnet took over from Billy Sutcliffe I, like all the other players, had certain reservations about the appointment because I knew he wouldn't be good enough as a batsman, bowler or a fielder. Now it's going to sound a bit crazy, but take away those three shortcomings (and obviously they are important ones to say the least) and Ronnie did an absolutely fantastic job for

Yorkshire cricket. On paper we shouldn't have been as good as we had been three or four years earlier, but he got us on the right lines and he did it by being a straight, honest, true man. One example of this affected me personally. Previous captains had tended to drop me down the order when one of the specialist batsmen was a bit out of form and wanted to go in lower down. In 1959 I was having a super season – I made five centuries – and Ken Taylor was having a bad time at number one. He dropped down to number five and then went back to opening again where he had another bad run, so he asked to go to number five again. I protested. 'Surely I'm not going to have to go back to number six or seven again because I am a bowler?' I said. Ronnie was quite straight about it. 'No', he said. 'If Ken wants to drop down the order, he'll go in at six, after you.' Ken had played with Ronnie in the second team and they were quite friendly, whereas I had never played with Ronnie before – but that didn't make any difference to him. He was fair, and that was Ronnie right through: a hundred per cent fair.

People say he made one or two mistakes. Well, perhaps he did, but he can't have made too many because we won the championship after ten years without winning anything. I thought he took good advice from the more experienced players, and I also thought he sorted it out very well for himself. Remember, we were a fairly inexperienced side with a lot of young players coming on and when you take that into account Ronnie did a fantastic job. He made everyone believe in himself and some of our scoring feats in 1959 were incredible. We've never got near them since. He got everyone playing for each other and playing like hell for Yorkshire, and that has stuck in my mind ever since. There can be no stars in a team game. Ronnie Burnet sowed the seeds of that philosophy in my mind more than any other man, and it is a philosophy I have never forgotten.

I had played with a team of internationals and a bad team spirit, and then I had played in a team with many of those internationals missing and a lot of inexperienced players in their places, but with a fantastic team spirit. The experience proved invaluable when I became a captain myself. When my time came I knew what was wanted.

Of my five centuries in that 1959 season the most important by far was the 122 against Sussex in an incredible last game of the season at Hove. We had to win the game to win the champion-ship, and Sussex took a terribly long time to get 210 in the first innings. I went in at 38 for three and we were 78 for four and 81 for five with time slipping by as well. It looked like goodbye to any hopes of the championship for another year. But as it had done so often that season, the marvellous team spirit asserted itself and two of the most inexperienced members of the side stayed with me – Jack Birkenshaw made 38 and then Don Wilson 55, and we had a first innings lead of 97. But that little bit of green that is usually around at Hove wasn't there in the second innings and it was a matter of winkling them out with the spinners.

At lunch on the third day, Sussex were nearly 200 ahead with three wickets left, and close of play was 4.30 p.m. Ian Thomson and some of the senior Sussex players wanted to declare but Robin Marlar wouldn't. With the championship at stake, his view was 'they'll have to bowl us out'. We did, a few overs after lunch, but to win the championship we had to score 215 in 103 minutes. It just didn't seem possible, but Ronnie insisted: 'We've got to go for them. We *can* get them.'

Well, the captain certainly inspired Bryan Stott because he hit the first ball of the innings straight over the sightscreen for six. I'll never forget that stroke as long as I live. After that it seemed as if everyone was inspired. Stottie and Doug Padgett took us to a position where Brian Bolus and I could just take it easy as we knocked off the few remaining runs. It was an unbelievable per-formance and understandably, that mad second innings dash took all the headlines; but I like to think that it was my first innings 122 which put us in a position to win. That's why it was my favourite century of that season. It was also very much a part of playing under Ronnie Burnet. He had created a team spirit without making any of us feel that we were under pressure. If we had stopped to analyse our feelings I think we would have said to ourselves: 'I am one of a good set of lads and we are going all out for everything.' It was something as simple and indefinable, really, as that. Ronnie had got us going. We believed in ourselves and we believed in each other, and without ostentatiously spelling anything out for us Ronnie had created, from a largely inexperi-enced party of players, a unit which was now a formidable team. We were no longer a collection of individuals pulling in all kinds of different directions. We pulled together.

I felt sorry for Ronnie in some ways when he was supplanted after the championship season of 1959, by Vic Wilson. It filtered through that a bit of pressure had been exerted by Brian Sellers, that Ronnie had done the job he had been given to do, that the team spirit (missing for so long) was now established, and that the Burnet mission was complete. With hindsight, it *might* have been the right decision. Certainly it made us stronger on the field in every way – batting, bowling and fielding – and, again, the team spirit was now there. Possibly, taking everything into account, it was the right decision. But I hope no one ever forgets just what Ronnie Burnet did for Yorkshire in an astonishingly short space of time. All right, he was not a gifted cricketer, but the trans-formation that occurred during his captaincy was not accidental.

Vic Wilson took over for the 1960 season as the first professional to be appointed as a Yorkshire captain. He was a very honest, straightforward, down-to-earth guy. I don't think he was the most imaginative of captains but he had always been a great bloke and a great team-man and because of that I think most people in the side would have done anything for him. He was captain for three seasons and Yorkshire finished first, second and first again. Now I think if almost anyone else had captained the side in that middle season we would have won the championship in 1961 as well, and it's also pretty certain that only a Yorkshireman would look at things that way. Two firsts and a second ... and we are left reflecting that the second should have been a first as well. If Vic had shown just a little more imagination, particularly towards the end of the season, I don't think we would have seen Hampshire win their first championship. But with two championships and a runner's-up place for Yorkshire, Vic Wilson can't have been all that bad a captain, can he?

Then came Closey. Well, I have talked about him at some length elsewhere in this book, but in the context of county captaincy he obviously rates very highly. When we were attacking he was a great captain, there's no doubt about that. He led by example, especially in the field.

He would sit on top of the bat, no matter who was batting ... the greatest hooker or cutter in the world could be there and Brian would be at short leg or silly point. He would move himself around, from one side to the other, and move other close fieldsmen for no reason that was immediately obvious. He would set out to make the batsman think, or ponder or worry ... to wonder whether something was happening that he couldn't, for that moment, spot. Closey applied pressure in a way that few captains before or afterwards, have ever applied it. As a batsman no one could intimidate him; as a bowler he bowled well either with the seam up or as a spinner, and sometimes with a mixture which no one could work out because, quite frankly, he didn't know himself. He was, as he used to put it, trying to 'fiddle' something and very often he did. More than once he got Ted Dexter out, at the height of his career, with a full toss; and Ted's fury was equalled only by Brian's glee. But it worked ... somehow it worked.

Now against that, Closey's temperament is pretty well known. He couldn't give absolute concentration for six hours a day. When the opposition were well set and things weren't going our way his attention tended to wander from time to time. Jimmy Binks would then come from behind the stumps at the end of an over and say: 'Hey up – t'rudder's gone again. Go and have a word with him.' Now Brian may have been cleverer than I thought. Maybe he knew that I was the sort of bloke who *could* keep concentrating the whole of the time and maybe he knew that I was keeping an eye on things and would come up with a suggestion. I don't know. But he did take notice of me when I said: 'Come on. This bloody situation is getting serious. Let's do this, or that, or something else.' He *would* listen.

I have mentioned the role of Jimmy Binks there, and apart from anything else he was part of the brains of the team which clustered round the wicket, watching the behaviour of every ball, every movement and every reaction of every batsman. One way or another, I like to think that very little escaped one or other of the Yorkshire hierarchy on the field. But Binky was a very fine wicket-keeper, too. I know that Alan Knott, for instance, feels that for a time Jimmy Binks was the finest wicket-keeper in the country. Between 1955 and 1969 he kept in 412 consecutive County Championship matches for Yorkshire. He played with broken fingers and a variety of other injuries, and yet he was always involved in every minute of every game.

But everyone has an off-day. Jimmy lived at Hull and played

in the days before motorways threaded their high-speed way across most of the country. Consequently, matches at Bradford, and Leeds and Sheffield, were virtually away games for him and so, after a day's play at Park Avenue, or Headingley, or Bramall Lane, he either went to a hotel for the night or stayed with one of the lads. During a Roses match at Headingley he was staying with me, and we were in with a chance if we could have got 'Noddy' Pullar out. It was a turning wicket but Noddy, in those days, had an average of over 70 in matches against Yorkshire and he took a delight in getting his runs off our bowling. It didn't matter how long he took; so long as he was there and we were getting more and more twitched up, the better he liked it. On this particular occasion Jimmy had missed him at least three times off me and that evening, when we went up to the local for a beer one of my friends came up to us at the bar and said: 'Bad luck, Raymond lad. If you'd had a bloody wicket-keeper we'd have had that match won by now.' With a certain amount of delight I asked him, 'You've met Jimmy Binks, have you?' We had a drink and a laugh together and then Jimmy and I went home. At the end of the night's television programmes the epilogue came on and Binky with hands together, prayed, 'Please, God, don't let me miss any more off Illy'. Next morning, needless to say, my first ball to Noddy turned, he got an edge and Binky put it down. All over the ground his voice was heard, 'Bugger the bloody epilogue'!

Part of our close-to-the-wicket team – indeed, a vital part – was Philip Sharpe, one of the greatest slip-catchers I have ever seen. I saw quite a bit of Simpson but to me, Sharpie was the greatest. His concentration was incredible. He could stand for five-and-a-half hours with nothing coming to him and then, in the last half hour, he would pull off the most breathtaking catch. Philip liked his social life, and had quite a few outside interests, so in the course of a day's play all kinds of thoughts must have passed through his mind. But the minute the bowler was into his delivery stride all other thoughts were dismissed and his concentration on the ball was absolute. I recall one game for England against the West Indies at Lord's when Sharpie had been at slip all day long without anything going his way at all. With five minutes to go John Shepherd pushed hard at one from me, aiming for the covers, and Sharpie took it full-length, right-handed. *That's* slip-fielding.

48

7
CAPPED BY YORKSHIRE AND ENGLAND

Those were the high politics of my playing career with Yorkshire. If they create the impression that life before 1959 was all misery and that from that year onwards all was sweetness and light, then that is misleading. I couldn't be miserable when I was playing cricket – and getting paid for doing so: never. No, it was simply that at that time I felt a good life could have been even better without the 'aggro' created by those hard men, and defeats could have been turned into victories by less selfishness and a good deal more cooperation. That great side of the 1950s never won anything because it wasn't a *team*, not because it was anything less than a great side. Surrey, with seven successive championships, were a splendid side and they were also a team. And although their players of the fifties deny it (none more vociferously than Alec Bedser and Jim Laker, who insist that their winning sequence was due purely and simply to their greater ability), everyone else in the game knew that they had the inestimable help of the groundsman, Bert Lock. As Surrey played all their home games on the one ground, The Oval, his was help of considerable magnitude. Bert was a magician who seemed able to prepare the sort of pitch as exactly suited to Surrey as it was disadvantageous to the opposition. If the visiting team were strong in seamers, they would find themselves on a spinner's paradise, with Laker and Tony Lock mowing them down. If a county arrived with spinning strength in depth, they would find Bedser and Loader rubbing their hands and itching to get into action with the far from negligible help of Stuart Surridge (who was also a good slip-catcher as well as a shrewd, tough captain). In the last analysis it is bowlers (and captains) who win matches because to win you have got to expect to bowl the other side out twice.

49

Nevertheless, Surrey didn't exactly walk all over us every year and we ran them very close on one or two occasions. In 1954, for instance, we were pushing them very hard and we would, in fact, have taken the title if we had won our last two games. We bowled Kent out cheaply in the first innings and they had five down in the second while still behind – and it rained all through the third day. We went on to Sussex, got them into an almost identical position, and again it rained throughout the third day. Surrey, meanwhile, won both matches in two days with Lock taking eight for 12 and seven for 12!

In the Kent match there had been another of those incidents which, as far as I could see, was suicide for a side trying to win a very tough competition. Fred Trueman had taken six wickets fairly cheaply when a batsman got a nick on to his pad, and the ball lobbed up to the backward short leg position where Johnny Wardle (who was a good close catcher) put the catch down. Now by pure coincidence, Fred and Johnny were in extremely close contention for a bowling award of £250, a lot of money in those days, given by the makers of Brylcreem; and without any ceremony whatsoever, F.S. accused Wardle of dropping the catch deliberately. There was what you might call 'a heated exchange' between the two, which did not exactly recede into the distance when, less than a week later, Wardle was judged to have just pipped Fred for the prize! I cannot really bring myself to believe that Johnny would deliberately drop a catch, but no one to this day has been able to convince Fred that he didn't!

While this sort of altercation continued to shatter what semblance of harmony there was in our ranks, I was quietly trying to learn my trade, to make myself more completely professional. I listened to what the senior players had to say, I studied opposition players, searching for flaws. My first championship century came in 1953, at Hull, when I was twenty. It was scored against Essex, and as three of my first four 'tons' came against that county, Trevor Bailey and I came to see rather a lot of each other. The *Bradford Telegraph & Argus* reported:

'No other century for years by a Yorkshire Colt has surpassed in merit Illingworth's effort which would have been an outstanding performance in any event but was made the more notable because it came at a time when the side was in a trying position. For the third time on successive days the team's leading batsmen had fallen all-too-readily and the position that Illingworth had to face was that Halliday, Hutton, Lester, Wilson and Watson all had been swept aside for a mere 104 in a surprising ascendancy by the Essex attack, with former England amateur Trevor Bailey as the spearhead.'

We declared at 366 for seven when I was 146 not out.

It was two years before I scored my next hundred, but that is not entirely surprising in view of the fact that I was batting at number six, seven or even eight behind the sort of talent which had been 'swept away' by Bailey and Co that Saturday morning in Hull. And don't forget that list did not include Frank Lowson and Brian Close, who also batted ahead of me. But as an all-rounder there was always a chance to do something with the ball and in the same year as that maiden century I took seven for 23 against Hampshire and six for 29 against Kent. I was learning

In 1955, I got my second first-class century (again against Essex) and was awarded my cap. I had arrived. The next game was against MCC at Scarborough on what was a bit of flier in the first hour (poor old Closey was bowled by the first delivery of the match and confessed that he never saw it) and I indulged in a little private celebration by hitting 138 out of 304. In 1956 I took 100 wickets for the first time and in 1957 came my first 'double' of 1,000 runs and 100 wickets.

My best bowling performance had stood since 1954 as eight for 69 against Surrey when I surpassed it at Worcester three years later, and again this put me in select company. My nine for 42 was achieved with Johnny Wardle bowling at the other end and I rated that in itself as no mean achievement – until the statisticians and historians came up with the news that only the great George Herbert Hirst had ever taken nine Worcestershire wickets for Yorkshire, nine for 41 on the same ground. But somewhere along the line, one statistician (the rather important one who keeps Yorkshire's official records up to date!) has given me even more credit. While all the reference books follow the newspapers of the day in listing my performance as nine for 42, the Yorkshire CCC Handbook, year after year, credits me with having taken the wickets for only *32*. Flattering, but wrong. I wonder why?

In 1958 I was called upon to stand by for the second Test against New Zealand at Lord's, and not unnaturally my hopes rose of a first England cap. Jim Laker had reported an injured spinning finger and I expected to play if Jim found he was unfit for duty. In those days Lord's was a bit of a green-top and he didn't play there very often, but on this occasion there was rain on the night before the game. Faced with the probability of a drying wicket, the Laker digit made a miraculous recovery to give him four for 13 in the first innings, one for 24 in the second, and New Zealand were bowled out for 47 and 74 to give England their second easy win of the series. So Laker naturally played in the next Test, taking five for 17 and three for 27 at Headingley, putting England three up in the series.

After that, perhaps with the winter tour to Australia in mind, the selectors decided to have a look at one or two less familiar faces, and I was picked for the Fourth Test at Old Trafford along with Ted Dexter and Ramon Subba Row. I scored three not out, took one for 39 in the first innings, two for 20 in the second and disappeared from the Test scene for the moment.

It was, perhaps, a mixed blessing, because Shirley and I had our marriage plans worked out and if I had been picked for the tour that winter the wedding would have had to be postponed. I've never asked Shirley whether she felt disappointed or relieved when the tour party was announced without my name on the list!

So I had to wait until the following summer for my next taste of Test cricket with D. K. Gaekwad's Indians as the tourists. Fred Trueman had murdered them on their previous visit, seven years earlier, and I suppose everyone remembers the scoreboard at Headingley in their second innings – nought for four – as well as Fred's figures at Old Trafford ... eight for 31. In 1959, I had to wait until the Fourth Test (Old Trafford again) before getting my chance. Martin Horton was played as the all-rounder spinner in the first two Tests, along with the leg-spin of Tommy Greenhough; and in the Third, at Headingley, Brian Close came in with John Mortimore. Close scored 27 runs in his only innings and took five for 53 in the match as well as holding four catches – but was dropped. His bad luck was my good fortune and I replaced him, to score 68 for once out, take three for 79 and hold three catches! There wasn't much in it, I suppose, but I stayed in the side for The Oval and got a place on the winter tour to the West Indies.

In fact, 1959 was a vintage year for me in that I hit four centuries (including 162 against the tourists at Sheffield), got back in the England side, but – most important of all – had a good season for Yorkshire in the year they at last got back the championship which, really, we regarded as our personal property, but which had gone to Surrey for the last seven long years. It was a triumph for the team spirit Ronnie Burnet had promoted, and if I labour a point which is made elsewhere in this book I make no apology. It was a relatively young side; it was most certainly lacking in experience; and Ronnie himself, at forty years of age, had less experience than anyone in the side of county championship cricket. Yet we won fourteen, lost seven and drew seven of our twenty-eight championship matches – giving us two more victories than Gloucestershire and Surrey, our nearest rivals. We took the title by just eight points.

That victory was only achieved seven minutes from the end of the last day of the last championship match of the season, when we had to score 215 in 103 minutes. In the first 20 minutes we got 50; the 100 went up in 43 minutes, 150 in 63, and in 95 minutes we were home by five wickets. 1 September, 1959, was one of the great days of my life, as I know it was for every man in that side.

At the end of the season we beat a strong MCC side in the Scarborough Festival (in what was, incidentally, Dickie Bird's last match for Yorkshire before joining Leicestershire) and then we won by 66 runs in the Champion County v the Rest of England match at The Oval – after following on and scoring 425 in our second innings! And I could look forward to my first tour – to the West Indies under Peter May.

8
HAPPIER DAYS ON THE CIRCUIT

The first time I ever saw Freddie Trueman he was bowling slow left-arm. I hadn't seen him at the Yorkshire nets because he more or less burst on to the scene from nowhere. It was on the school-boys' (Yorkshire Federation) tour and we were having a bit of a practice before the game. He was bowling slow left-arm and he had a beautiful action! So when the game started and this bloke was given the job of opening the bowling I wondered what was happening: and when he ran in and bowled right arm fast, I was amazed! That is my first and lasting memory of F. S. Trueman. He was also the worst batsman I have ever seen when he first started. If you bowled him four straight balls you could absolutely guarantee that three would knock his hob down. He was hopeless, so it's quite amazing how much he developed and what a fine striker of the ball he became.

I did not have a lot to do with him in his early days because his National Service was deferred for a couple of years. When he went in to do his stint, I was finishing mine, so I didn't see much of him for another couple of years. When we were both in the England side I roomed with him sometimes but even then I didn't see much of him. He tended to go to bed later than me and I got up in the morning before him. I would pour him a cup of tea, tell him I was going down to breakfast, and leave him to it. Very few people ever saw Fred emerge for breakfast in his twenty years in the game! He fairly quickly cured me of driving with him because of his unpunctuality. We would arrange to meet at noon; when he hadn't arrived at two p.m. a 'phone call to his home would invariably find him still there: 'I'm just having a new tyre put on the back, sunshine. Shalln't be long.' He was in York, I was in Pudsey and we had about a hundred miles to drive. Not really to be relied upon, our Fred.

Apart from being a great bowler, he brought immense psychological advantages to the side because he spent very little time in our dressing-room. He was almost always to be found in the opposition's, and on the first morning of a game he would spread alarm and despondency amongst the less experienced members of their side. Lounging back in his seat and assuming the lordly air which he felt was natural to the most feared fast bowler of his day, he would stab a finger in the direction of one player after another and with quite sublime conviction he would announce: 'Well, there's one theer, and another theer and another theer – that's three for a start.' And he meant it! If it sounded a trifle boastful, the important thing was that the opposition believed what he said. I have seen young players come out to face Fred who, quite clearly, were literally terrified. He so obviously believed in his own invincibility that he just didn't give a damn what anyone else thought. That was what enabled him to hold his own amongst the 'hard men' in the side – Hutton, Appleyard, Wardle. They got both barrels straight between the eyes in any dust-up with Fred and they were *very* hard men. Of course, he had the additional advantage of being the number one shock bowler. We needed him and he knew we needed him, and it gave him a great advantage. But he was always a bit of a loner, rarely joining us for a drink in the evening, usually off on some errand of his own.

Wardle and Watson were members of the dressing-room bridge school with the relatively mild-mannered Vic Wilson and Ted Lester making up the four. It is a game which fascinated me from the first because of the degree of skill involved, and because the average English summer provides plenty of opportunity for playing. I learned by watching the other four rather than by reading up the fairly extensive literature of the game and later I was one of a regular four of our own with Brian Close as my partner – not an ideal partnership. I would leave Closey with a stone-cold certain four spades and go for a walk only to return to find he had gone two down. Once when it happened I asked him how the hell he could possibly have failed to make the contract and he gave that infuriating, silly little laugh of his and replied, 'I lost interest in the middle'. That was one of the occasions when

I went a little further than simply telling him to get stuffed!

But the Wardle–Watson menage could be an entertainment in itself, quite apart from the bridge. Johnny was a good player; his partner, Vic Wilson, wasn't quite so expert and occasionally he drove Wardle to high fury by leading from a doubleton. In the days when we travelled by train from one game to another I've seen Wardle throw the cards out of the window before snarling at his partner, 'How many more bloody times do I have to tell you *not* to lead from a doubleton?' And that would be the end of bridge for that trip.

Appleyard was a hard man, too, and it was our travelling by train which enabled Eddie Leadbeater (the leg-spinner who later went to Warwickshire) to get a sweet taste of revenge over Robert. He had been giving Eddie a particularly hard time as twelfth man and at the end of the game it was Eddie's job to take the team's cases to Leeds Station and to load them on to the train.

At the next platform to the London train stood one bound for Edinburgh, and after loading eleven bags on to one train Eddie, with a grim smile, put the twelfth on to the other. Naturally enough, when we arrived in London, 'Applecart' had no kit. He had to play next day in borrowed gear and if he reads this it will, I am sure, be the first intimation he has had of why his kit alone travelled to Edinburgh in 1951. Appleyard, Wardle, and Hutton formed an internal triangle which could make life distinctly unpleasant for young players and when I was involved I either kept quiet or got out of the way. Fred was a stronger character than the shy Raymond Illingworth. He gave back as good as he got, always.

There really was an awful lot of talent in that Yorkshire dressing-room of the earlier fifties. Sadly, there was not an awful lot of cameraderie. As I have said, in spite of the high level of ability, from the shared championship in 1949 to the outright win ten years later, that Yorkshire side never won a thing. What a different story it was during the next ten years despite Test calls which at one time or another took away Fred, Closey, myself, Geoff Boycott, Philip Sharpe, Doug Padgett, and Ken Taylor. I believe I played at a good time. There were good quick bowlers, some good spinners, some fine batsmen. Competition was fierce but there was a spirit within the game which had not existed in my own dressing-room in the early part of my career and which I don't feel exists in the game as a whole today.

We played two three-day games a week and so we knew that we would be travelling, all things being equal, each Tuesday and Friday night through the summer. There were some pretty hairy journeys – Leeds to Swansea, Clacton to Scarborough, Lord's to Middlesbrough – but we travelled more or less in convoy, stopping for a meal together, and there was always the probability of another Close driving story for the repertoire when we reached each destination. In fact, without the network of motorways now spread over the country we most of us had an adventure or two on those twice weekly trips. Once, leaving Northampton on one of the awkward cross-country journeys, someone announced that he knew a shortcut and led a posse of cars on a tortuous route through a series of winding country lanes. Suddenly we came upon the tightest of corners and no one managed to negotiate it successfully. Fortunately, however, there was a farmyard which acted as an escape road. All of a sudden, a farmer living miles from anywhere found three Yorkshire cars in his yard, covered in hens and ducks all squawking in righteous indignation at this noisy and un-expected disruption of their rural tranquillity.

My travelling companion and room-mate in those days was Dougie Padgett, another friend of my youth. He had been called to the nets about the same time as me although he was a couple of years younger, and we used to meet at the bus stop and travel together to Headingley. He, too, played in the Bradford League, with Idle, so in a cricketing sense we had grown up together. We had a great personal liking for each other which manifested itself in a perhaps characteristically West Riding fashion, by a whole catalogue of complaints about one another's various traits or habits. (If anyone had dared to moan to either of us about the other, he would have been in trouble, but to savage each other's characters was legitimate, because we both knew that – para-doxically, perhaps, to the outsider – the moans were born of a basic affection for, and understanding of, each other.)

Padgie was, for instance, a great sleeper anywhere except in his bed. He could get his head down in the noisiest dressing-room or when the car was being driven through the thickest traffic. Neither did he believe in doing any of the driving unless he was absolutely forced into it. He has got into the car at the start of a trip from, say, Park Avenue to Cardiff, and been fast asleep inside five minutes. So I used to combat this by driving with the offside wheels vibrating over the cat's-eyes, and even Doug couldn't sleep through that for very long. Once in bed, however, it was a different story. He was a compulsive walker, and talker, in his sleep. He would leap up in the middle of the night roaring appeals, waving his arms about and holding *fortissimo* conversations with people who weren't there. Once, in Oxford, I found him at the window shouting down into an empty street, 'Come up, Finney. Finney, come on'. He had spent his National Service in the army with Alan Finney and Albert Quixall, two Sheffield Wednesday footballers, and clearly they had had one or two nocturnal adventures together which had planted themselves deep in Doug's sub-conscious.

In the Yorkshire dressing-room each morning there was a session known as 'the notice board' – when details were given of anything out of the ordinary which had happened the night before to anyone in what was, let's face it, a rather colourful collection of personalities. Padgie could usually be relied upon to supply an item, or at least his exploits could. The essence of it all was to give everyone a laugh.

That was a fun session, not a time of bitching. It was an atmosphere which could only be created by a happy side which was basically a group of friends. As I have said, we were each of us rather colourful personalities either in the playing sense, or the personal sense, or both, yet we went into action together as a unit. No one was bigger than the team; no one was more important than anyone else. Everyone had a job to do and we knew that if everyone did that job properly there was more than enough ability for us to win games and, in due course, the championship. I am not trying to say that there was never a moment of disagreement, on the personal level or about what should be done in certain playing situations. Occasionally some of us had quite different ideas and occasionally some of us said so. But none of it was left to rankle. There was none of the feuding or brooding resentment or petty jealousy that I had seen in the fifties. If we had a row, that was it and tomorrow was another day. If we lost a game, we knew why we had lost it and no one had to say, 'We are not going to make the same mistake again'.

We all knew we wouldn't. That was what it was like to play in a team ... a good team.

One of the eternal problems of the average first-class cricketer is to find a suitable job between seasons. It was even more of a problem twenty and thirty years ago when the rewards for a season of cricket were not as high as they are today, even though the pound was worth a pound. There were nothing like as many fringe benefits as there are today in the form of bonuses, talent money, endorsements for advertising, writing and speaking. It had to be a pretty benevolent employer who would keep a job open for four months a year and at a time when he was going to be short-staffed because of holidays. Benevolent employers like that, who could provide an enjoyable and lucrative job, were very few and far between. An additional problem for me was a lack of self-confidence when I was asked to do something with which I was not familiar. I was all right on a cricket field because I had grown up with my developing ability, and I knew I could do that job satisfactorily. But when I got a job selling fireworks and Christmas cards in Scotland, working from a base in Leeds, the boss asked me to work on a commission-only basis. Never having worked as a salesman before I did not have enough confidence in myself to accept this and I said I would prefer a wage and some commission. He said he would prefer me to work on commission, but would guarantee me minimum earnings and in fact I earned in commission just about the amount he had guaranteed me.

Once I had done the job, I then found the confidence I needed and agreed the following year to work again – on a commission-only basis. I doubled my earnings from the previous year. The job itself may sound strange, perhaps, but Scotland has long been the best selling-area for that firm because the Scots buy fireworks two or three times a year for different celebrations – not the big display items but simply the type that kids enjoy round the bonfire on Guy Fawkes' Night in England. And I got on well with the Scots, first in the border counties and then further north in Fife, Perthshire and Angus. I found the Scots very much like Yorkshire people in many ways, and up to two or three years ago I was very lucky with the weather. I had always made my trips up there in January and rarely seen any snow, but then I got caught in a blizzard and went off the road between Brechin and Forfar. On the same day Bob White (of Nottinghamshire), on a similar sales expedition in Aberdeenshire, went off his road as well. In the 1977–78 winter I just missed the bad weather – in fact I saw it coming so I made a quick dash into Aberfeldy, made my call there, and got out of the hills as quickly as I could. During the following week almost everyone in that area was stuck in cars, buses and trains – snowbound.

Except when I have been on tour, of course, this has been my winter job for the past sixteen or seventeen years. Before that I had done a winter with my father in the cabinet-making business, I had been in cloth, in chemical dyestuffs, and even spent one winter on the greenkeeping staff of Fulneck Golf Club. But, as I have said, it is not easy getting the right sort of job and many cricketers still struggle to find one between seasons. Cricketers probably enjoy their work more than most people and I am sure they get more pleasure out of it than other professional sportsmen. But that doesn't pay the mortgage or the electricity bill. It is a painful fact of life that a Yorkshire cricketer before the war was very much better off than present-day players in terms of income and in terms of prestige within the community.

9
THOUGHTS ON CAPTAINCY

I did not, by any stretch of the imagination, have a successful tour of the West Indies, although I played in all five Tests, but as I was still trying to learn something from every day's cricket, the experience was not wasted.

When Peter May had to fly home because of illness I had my first taste of Colin Cowdrey's captaincy in the last two matches. More important, I was just a little surprised to find that the distinction between amateur and professional players was, if anything, even more pronounced on tour than it was at home. I had grown up with the system as a county cricketer in England and while I accepted it (as we all did), as the natural order of things in the game we had made our career, it nevertheless did not prevent my reflecting from time to time that it was a far from ideal situation.

With Yorkshire, we were all expected to book our own accommodation and so, playing at Lord's for instance, half a dozen of us would end up in the Portland Arms (a large pub, in effect, handy for the ground), with Len Hutton on his own at the Great Western, Willie Watson, perhaps, in yet another place, and the amateurs enjoying rather more salubrious hospitality in London's West End. That didn't seem to me to be tremendously good for team spirit.

For the county match at Scarborough, we used a homely boarding-house run by a certain Mrs Hogg, who was as good as gold in keeping a few rooms available for as many of us as possible until the very last minute. But at Scarborough in July, good, reasonably-priced accommodation was snapped up quickly. We were never sure at that stage of our careers whether we would be picked or not so there were occasional last-minute bids for whatever room Mrs Hogg had left. This led, in one game, to the highly interesting combination of F. S. Trueman, Frank Lowson and Eddie Leadbeater sharing a double bed! Strange bedfellows indeed ... all had quite different social habits and kept widely different hours, so none of them got very much unbroken sleep!

At the Festival we were usually accommodated at The Salisbury, a pleasant, rather quiet establishment which described itself – reasonably, I think – as 'a family hotel', while the amateurs lived in palatial splendour at The Grand. If we wanted a glimpse of how the other half lived, we could walk a couple of hundred yards down the road to see our 'unpaid' colleagues taking dinner, resplendent in black tie! On the 1962–63 tour to Australia this was, I think, brought home to me even more forcibly than in the West Indies because there, as amateurs, we had the Bishop of Liverpool (then in his less exalted role of the Reverend David Sheppard), 'Lord Edward' Dexter, Colin Cowdrey and A. C. Smith and they were to be found, nightly, dining with our manager, His Grace the Duke of Norfolk. Very occasionally, one of the pros was invited to join them. If five cars were laid on as team transport, more often than not the pros found themselves in one while the amateurs contrived as far as possible to bag one each. I don't think we would have minded quite so much if we hadn't been acutely conscious of the fact that some amateurs were getting a good deal more out of the game than the pros. There were rather a lot of shamateurs around at that time.

I do not think I had, at that stage, any visions of skippering England myself. I was not even anywhere near being captain of Yorkshire, where they were still some way from appointing their first professional leader. But I'm quite sure I ruminated occasionally on the unsatisfactory nature of touring in a party which, by the very nature of its composition and the time-hallowed canons of social distinction, was bound to be split up into different cliques. In the long run it must have affected my thinking about leadership, and in particular tour leadership. When my time came, the philosophy was that everyone had to give one hundred per cent for everyone else and that was of paramount importance.

That was not, frankly, the policy which seemed to me to be followed by all the England captains under whom I served. My first, as I have said, was Peter May, a man I rated very, very highly indeed. He was a tremendous player – probably the best England have produced since the war. His boyish, almost diffident appearance on the field belied his real character because he was quite a hard man. His background was pure 'establishment' yet his approach to the game was highly professional. Perhaps that was developed through being brought up, so to speak, under Stuart Surridge with Surrey, and Len Hutton with England ... whatever the reasons, P. B. H. May was a tough skipper. Early in my career I remember playing on a wet wicket against New Zealand at Old Trafford with Peter saying, 'Come on now. Get stuck in', and really meaning it. Not the sort of attitude one really expected from the public school and university background that he had. And yet he was, for my money, a gentleman in the best sense of the word – a man I really admired. I was more than sorry when he retired.

Colin Cowdrey was the next, and from my point of view he could never make his mind up whether to call heads or tails. That just about sums up his captaincy. He never seemed able to make a decision about anything, he never had the courage of his convictions, and he had to be talked into things. Colin was vice-captain to Ted Dexter on my first tour of Australia and I had one or two 'dos' with him then, notably about his arriving for nets an hour after everyone else. Then there was an occasion when David Shepherd and I had been ill in hospital. I turned up at Melbourne after a week in a sick-bed and Colin asked me to do the twelfth man's duties. I told him: 'I don't feel like spending a day in the field if that becomes necessary; I've just been in hospital for a week. I'll do the dressing-room duties.' But Colin insisted: 'You've got to do the whole thing; we've nobody else available.' He, in fact, was taking his wife to the pictures to see the premiere of *Mutiny on the Bounty*. Someone did break down, and I had to do three-and-a-half hours in the field with the temperature over a hundred degrees which wasn't, I felt, the ideal convalescence.

Cowdrey went to Australia as my vice-captain on the 1970–71 tour and unfortunately did not carry out his duties in the way I had hoped and, indeed, expected. The first few weeks of a tour are pressingly busy for a captain. He is involved in all kinds of social invitations, both immediately and in prospect ... and has to decide when to accept and when to call enough. He is expected to be available not only to the British press (and that's a big party, all of them understandably wanting their own original story each day) but to the Australian press as well. There are television and radio boys wanting *their* own thing, and that usually involves a bit of travelling to a studio or hanging about for a fair length of time while elaborate gear is set up. It's a really busy time and comes when the all-important thing is to be keeping an eye on your tour party – is everybody reasonably comfortable? Are there any potentially fractious room-pairings? Is anybody homesick, unfit or unwell? So it is a time when a vice-captain really needs to be a man giving solid support to his captain.

At the start of that tour there were days when Cowdrey didn't even turn up at all at the nets: I expected him to be *organising* the nets. I asked the manager, David Clark (a Kent man himself) where Colin was and he didn't know. On occasions when Cowdrey did come to the nets, he would disappear as soon as the last ball was bowled and we wouldn't see him again that day. Obviously, he had been on five previous tours and knew a lot of people in Australia. He seemed to be determined to get round and see them all, which in other circumstances might have been acceptable but that was not at all what I expected from my vice-captain. Consequently I was more than grateful that Geoff Boycott and John Edrich – both experienced and thoroughly professional men – spotted my difficulties and volunteered to organise the nets.

Colin, over many distinguished cricketing years, has cultivated a public image of an affable, urbane, approachable chap who habitually wears a friendly smile for the world. Anyone meeting him for the first time would very naturally go away with the impression: 'What a nice fellow.' I accept that without question. Yet he was not generally liked by cricketers.

Ted Dexter was a man with whom I always got on well. He was a man's man. If you felt something was wrong you could tell him so, and he would accept it. I don't think he was ever a great captain because he hadn't the powers of concentration that captaincy requires. It's a six-hours-a-day job on the field, and then you often feel the work is just starting. But whilst you are playing, the captain's concentration has to be one hundred per cent. Ted was in an even higher league than Closey when it came to the 'drifting-off' stakes. He's a superb golfer, and quite often

Left: A future England Captain? Me aged four with our family dog, Peter.

Below: Wedding day, Farsley Parish Church, 1958, and a rare glimpse of my best man *almost* smiling. (Bradford and District Newspaper Co. Ltd)

Overleaf: Captain for the first time at Lord's. The high-stepping Peter Parfitt helps me lead out England *v* West Indies, 1969. (Sport & General)

Left: A new coin for a new captain to toss, 1969.

Below: My finest hour - victory over Gary Sobers's West Indies side at Headingley, 1969. (Central Press Photos)

Right: The toss with Graham Dowling - *v* New Zealand, Lord's 1969. (Sport & General)

Below right: HM The Queen on her traditional visit to Lord's. (Sport & General)

Left: A fairly confident appeal, and Mushtaq Mohammed is out lbw. England *v* Rest of the World, Headingley, 1970. (Sport & General)

Above: Victory over Pakistan at Headingley, 1971; I share the souvenir stumps with Geoff Boycott and Norman Gifford. (Sport & General)

Right: Approval from Richard Hutton and Alan Knott for a catch to dismiss Farokh Engineer; Lord's, 1971. (Sport & General)

Above: Engineer again, but this time he watches four runs to long leg. Old Trafford, 1971. (Central Press Photos)

Left: Ian Chappell has a glimpse of the Ashes at Lord's, 1972, but they stayed with England after a tied series. (Sport & General)

he would be miles away playing a quite marvellous eight-iron shot to the green when the ball was on its way to him in the gully . . . A good bloke, Ted, but not a great captain in my opinion.

Closey I've dealt with, so where do I rate myself in this dynasty? Basically, I felt my two strongest points were first, after playing for quite a time I knew batsmen pretty well and I knew their temperaments so I thought I set good fields; and second, I think I was able to get the best out of people because they trusted me.

I knew when to attack and when to defend, which governed field-placing, and my handling of the bowling. And in the other context, players knew that they could talk to me, could ask me things, and they knew they would get an honest answer. During the Rest of the World series before we went to Australia, Brian Luckhurst approached me and said he would like to ask me a question. 'Of course', I said, 'you know you can do that.' 'Well', said Brian, 'I wouldn't ask some people this because I don't think I'd get an answer, but what chance have I of going to Australia?' I told him: 'You are almost on the boat now. If you can make a couple of scores in the next two matches of this series you'll be there.' Now what I liked about that was that Brian had played only three matches with me, and yet he felt that not only could he ask such a question, but he was reasonably sure he'd get an honest answer. What, you may ask, would I have said if the answer had been that he was *not* in line for a tour place? It's a fair question, but I am quite sure my answer would have been just as straight and honest.

This has always been a matter of the greatest importance to me – honesty. I wouldn't have told him, 'You've no bloody chance'. I like to think it is possible to be less brutal than that while still being sincere, but I would have told him straight that his chances were slim, or even less than that.

Not every problem between captain and player is as relatively straightforward and easy to deal with as that. John Snow was certainly not an uncomplicated character and in my first Test as England captain – against the West Indies at Old Trafford – we had scored over 400 and bowled them out within the follow-on limit. Snow did not want to enforce the follow-on; I did, for the simple reason that there was unsettled weather about and I was sure we were going to lose some time. Snow had not done much bowling that day ... about ten or eleven overs ... and I had saved him for a particular purpose. West Indies reached 90 for none in the second innings when Basil D'Oliveira got a break-through for us so I said to Snowy: 'Come on, now. I want four quick overs from you. That's only 15 in the day. Let it go a bit.' He came in and gave us one of his military-medium sessions.

Then I stuck my neck out after only my first Test as England's captain. I said he didn't play in the next match – or I didn't. To be fair, the selectors backed me up. The only thing they didn't do was tell Snowy *why* he had been left out. When the team was announced he rang me up and asked why he was not selected. I told him, 'It is not my job to tell you that but I will have a word with the chairman of selectors and if he doesn't give you an explanation, I'll call you back and tell you myself'. I then rang Donald Carr at Lord's and said there was no point in leaving players out of Test sides, especially in circumstances like that, if they were not told why. He agreed, spoke to Alec Bedser, and Alec went down to Hove the following day to tell Snow. That was Snow's first match with me. He knew where he stood: and John Snow did not play in the next Test.

The scene now switches to Adelaide – the first state match on the tour of Australia that winter. Snow doesn't have weight problems like many fast bowlers have had and, in some cases, always will have. Some big men are built sparely, some tend to put on weight if they look at a pint of beer at the other end of the bar. Snowy was not one of these. So I had said to him: 'It's up to you to get yourself fit to bowl the way you've got to bowl on this tour. You know what you have to do to achieve that; I am going to leave it to you.'

Snow is an intelligent man. I had made my views very plain at Old Trafford during the series at home, and I didn't think it was necessary to labour the point. I expected Snowy to approach his tour in the same way that I expected everyone else to do it. I wanted to win the series and I didn't think it unreasonable to expect everyone else to feel the same way and to work for it accordingly.

During the South Australia first innings, Snow was going through the old, lethargic routine ... ambling gently round the third-man boundary and giving the Aussies three when it should have been one. In no time at all Pete Lever and some of the others were muttering darkly: 'What the hell's going on? Why are we tearing about cutting off runs when that so-and-so is giving them away?' At close of play I asked Snow to my room and my first words to him were: 'Snowy, if you weren't an intelligent bloke, you'd now be on the boat home. Because you *are* intelligent I am going to talk to you as someone who, I hope, can understand what I am trying to say to you.'

Then I told him: 'I have said you can get yourself fit in your own way and although I don't agree with your approach – you sometimes let a nine-ten-jack smash you back over your head – all right, I'll take that. I think you ought to show a bit of fire, a bit of resentment when that happens. If you don't mind it, I'll accept that. But I want you right for the Tests, make no mistake about that. In the meantime what you have got to realise is this: I can't have you wandering around at third man, or wherever it is, letting the batsmen take three when it should be one. I've got bowlers at the other end who watch this and their attitude is naturally going to be: "Why should I bowl my guts out when Snowy is treating it like a benefit match?" They are going to say, "If he's not trying, I'm not trying". Before long I'm going to have no one trying and then I'm nowhere at all. Now, do you see this Snowy? I am talking to you as an intelligent man' (I emphasised that) 'do you see what I am getting at?'

He accepted what I said, and next day he went out and really tried in the field. As we came off I said to him, 'Thanks, Snowy. That's all I wanted'. And from that day we were as right as rain. We understood each other. John knew that I was willing to stand up and fight for him (as I did on numerous occasions), but he had to fight for me as well.

That is captaincy as I understand it. You have to fight like hell – for each other. You have to give everything you have got – for each other. Star players are stars only within the firmament of the team. The team is what matters and the captain's job is to get that team together and one hundred per cent behind him. Sometimes you have to be tough; at times you have to be merciless. You have, in turn, to be compassionate and understanding. But above all you have to be the boss. You have to think *for* everyone at the same time as you are thinking *about* everyone – and studying the opposition as well. There's no time for thinking about what you are going to do on a rest day or at the weekend; there isn't even much time for giving a passing thought to what you are going to say in a speech that evening. You have to walk the tightrope between handing out a rollicking and showing a sympathetic understanding. You have to make decisions with thirty thousand people watching and wondering why you are making them. You have millions more watching television, listening to radio and, next day, reading the paper where (without any doubt) a number of armchair critics will have found that you were out of your mind to make a bowling change, a fielding position switch or a decision to bat or field. It's a lonely job – lonely as hell. The results of one single thought you might have are going to be in the record books for all time, and figures in cold print can never reflect all the heart-searching you put into that decision. But you are there to make the decisions, and with all the good advice in the world you are still the man who has to say the word. It is glorious power; it is terrifying responsibility.

10
CAPTAIN OF ENGLAND

In June, 1969, Colin Milburn was badly injured in a road accident one evening after a day's play with Northamptonshire and the dreadful report we read next morning was that he would probably lose an eye. The following evening, on finishing a game at Leicester, Graeme McKenzie and I called to see Ollie in hospital on our way to the next game at Hove. He must have known that his injuries were bound to spell the end of a career which had made him one of the most popular men in the game, but he gave no hint of this. He was quite amazingly cheerful – in fact just the same jolly, irrepressible Milburn we all knew. So we felt just a bit better as we drove southwards than we had when we first heard about the crash. On our arrival at the Imperial Hotel we found an army of television cameras, newspaper men and radio reporters, waiting on the doorstep. As we had driven from Leicester, the selectors had announced that I was to captain England in the First Test against the West Indies. They must, in fact, have tried to contact me at Grace Road shortly after I left and then, of course, there was no contact with me until I reached Brighton.

The news came more as a relief than a surprise because, of course, speculation had been rife for some weeks. Colin Cowdrey, the 'sitting tenant' in the captaincy, had snapped an Achilles tendon and although there was no doubt in my mind that he would get the captaincy if he was fit, there was obviously a chance that I would get it if he were not. Of the other candidates, I felt Tom Graveney had the best chance because of his experience, and his vice-captaincy to Cowdrey in three previous series. On the other hand, I felt that Tom might not be an entirely unanimous choice

69

of certain selectors and therefore I had spent the last couple of weeks with the idea that I had a pretty fair chance. All the same it felt good ... very good indeed ... to know that at last it was official. I had come a long way from Wesley Street School and Farsley's second team. I was thirty-seven, with thirty Tests and two tours behind me, and though I was in my first season as captain of Leicestershire I was confident I knew enough about the game to do a good job. With a snapped Achilles tendon I could not see Cowdrey being fit enough to play at all that season; and although there was no doubt in my mind that he would be restored to the captaincy as soon as he was fit again, I wanted to concentrate now on doing the best possible job that summer. I was confident without being cocky – I hope I have never appeared cocky to anyone. But I did feel confident. This was based on my feeling that the players knew enough about me to trust me to make the right decisions.

I had been appointed, initially, for only one Test and thus from a personal standpoint, as well as England's, it was particularly important to do well. (In fact all through my career as Test captain I was appointed for one, two or three Tests at a time – never a full five-Test series. I hope I shall be forgiven my wry smile ten years later at seeing Brearley appointed for one full series after another.

So I was as relieved as I was happy to win the First Test at Old Trafford by ten wickets, helped, I like to think, by winning the toss with a newly-minted fifty pence piece given to me by my friendly neighbourhood Midland Bank manager in Pudsey for that purpose. We scored 413 and 12 without loss, bowling out the West Indies for 147 and 275. After that win I was given the captaincy for the next two Tests but the coin didn't help me at Lord's – West Indies scored 380. We were then really in the cart after losing four cheap wickets and the moment had arrived for my first Test 100. It gave me the most enormous pleasure to have John Hampshire at the other end making a century in his first Test. So from a position of disaster we finished only 36 behind on the first innings and were able to draw the Test after being 331 behind when we had to bat last. In fact we were in with a chance of winning until we lost two or three wickets after tea on the final day, and then had to save the game. And so to Headingley, and what I have always regarded as my finest match as England's captain. Bringing back the Ashes from Australia, two years later, was obviously one of the great thrills of my life, and there have, of course, been other highlights. But in simple terms of organising a side and pitting my wits and experience against the opposition, of containing then attacking the other side as the occasion demanded, of making the bowling and field-placing changes that were called for, of all round, thinking, captaincy, then Headingley 1969 was my finest hour.

The pitch was green in the early stages, and then got progressively easier as the game went on. We scored 223 and bowled the Windies out for 161. We then added 240, which left them needing 303 to win. As I have said, the wicket got better and better, and with their batting line-up, and plenty of time, the target was far from impossible. At 177 for three it looked, on paper, as though the odds were against us, with Basil Butcher and Steve Camacho going well. But we had thought a lot about our cricket and had worked out a number of ploys in attacking the weaknesses of certain individual players.

Consequently, even when they wanted only 126 to win with seven wickets in hand (some of them very good wickets) I didn't feel we had lost command of the game. Neither, apparently, did Basil D'Oliveira, because he was asked afterwards by the veteran cricket-writer, Reg Hayter, if he felt the match was lost at that point. He was kind enough to reply: 'No. If they had got 30 or 40 more runs then I would have said it had gone, but at that stage I felt Illy was still on top of his job and we were still dictating the course of the game.'

We got rid of Camacho, finally, and then were ready and waiting for Gary Sobers, because we had worked out something special for him. This involved bowling a wide half-volley to him – a good two feet wide. Our reasoning was that Gary would be unable to resist such a ball, even though it was really too wide to hit in the middle of the bat. We had the bowler to put it just where we wanted it in Barry Knight, and exactly the right slip-catcher in Philip Sharpe. It had worked at Old Trafford in the first Test and it had worked again in the first innings at Headingley. So when Gary came in, on came Knight. By this time I am quite sure Gary knew what we were trying to do but I read him as regarding it as a challenge. Sobers was such a great player that I felt it was ninety-nine per cent certain that he would try to show us that he could beat any trap we set for him. Sure enough, he got right across to Knight's wide half-volley – far enough this time to make sure he didn't get the outside edge for which Sharpe was waiting. He got so far across that he got an *inside* edge and nicked it on to his wicket ... 'Sobers b Knight o'! I took Underwood off at a time when he had just taken a wicket which didn't please him, but Clive Lloyd had just come in and at that time I didn't regard Derek as a good bowler at left-handers. In fact I thought he was a *bad* bowler at left-handers, especially after watching Bob Cowper, the Australian, cut him to pieces. So I took over myself, got Lloyd's wicket and brought Underwood straight back. That worked, and we took the new ball at just the right time to polish off the tail and win by 30 runs.

It was one of those days when everything worked out right but it wasn't just a series of accidents or pieces of good luck. I don't think we were given sufficient credit by quite a lot of people for the amount of thought we had given to playing that opposition. Our method of attacking Sobers destroyed him in that series to such an extent that a prominent section of the press wrote him off as finished. When he returned to play several more tremendous Tests I never noticed those writers reflecting that there might have been a reason for his 1969 failures other than loss of form.

But Ray Robinson, the distinguished Australian writer, did analyse what had happened. He wrote to me afterwards with a questionnaire, asking what I felt at certain times, what pressures were on me, why I had made various bowling changes at particular times, and he prefaced his questions with the comment that this was one of the finest bits of captaincy he had ever seen. Now that was gratifying, not because I lap up praise as such – I don't – but because the detailed nature of the questionnaire showed that Ray, at least, knew that a great deal of thought, care and preparation had gone into England's performance in the field that day.

Two wins and one draw against the West Indies inspired the selectors with enough confidence to appoint me for the three Tests against New Zealand. Again we won two and drew the other, after which we played, in 1970, five matches against a Rest of the World team in place of what should have been a tour by South Africa.

I was given the captaincy in the first, then the second, then the third, and after that the selectors really had to make their minds up about who was going to be captain in Australia during the winter. Although we lost four and won only one of the series against that powerful Rest of the World side (which, ironically, included South Africans even though they weren't allowed to come as a team – what a lot of hypocrisy there is in this tragically continuing saga of excluding South African teams from international sport!), it seemed ridiculous to me to find the captaincy doled out grudgingly in this way. There was the usual lobby in the usual quarters for Cowdrey to return as captain for the Australian tour but I didn't get really worried about it. I felt I had had a good summer against West Indies and New Zealand and if there was any justice around I would get the job. I have heard that when I did get the appointment it was on a three-one vote by the selectors with Don Kenyon, Billy Sutcliffe and A. C. Smith voting for me and Alec Bedser going for Cowdrey. I have never been able to establish this with absolute certainty, but I have very strong reasons for believing it to be correct.

In view of what is regarded as the success of the Bedser–Illingworth era, I find this rather ironical. Be that as it may, I had just come in from batting (one of my six successive scores of 50 or more to equal a Denis Compton record) at Edgbaston, when Big Al came into the dressing-room and said, 'Well played. I'd just like to tell you that you've got the job for Australia'. In the next breath he added, 'And we've invited Colin to be vice-captain'.

Now it wasn't really the ideal time to spring all this upon me. I still had my pads on; my mind was still full of the concentration required to bat for around two-and-a-half hours against the best bowlers in the world. I wasn't entirely 'with it'. I know I experienced a feeling of sheer delight at the thought that I was going to lead England in Australia – it was what I had always dreamed of doing – but the rest didn't really sink in. So when Alec went on, 'That's all right with you, isn't it?', I hadn't even given the vice-captaincy a thought. Still thinking what it meant to me to be captain, I replied, 'Yes, I suppose it's all right with me'. The news was then released to the press, and once that had been done there was no going back. On reflection, I would rather have had time to consider the implications in cooler, calmer circumstances.

Cowdrey then took weeks to make his mind up. Time passed without any word of acceptance from him, and the selectors asked me to write a letter to him, suggesting that he should accept the vice-captaincy, saying I appreciated that we had had differences in the past but that I was willing to put these behind me and I hoped he was willing to do so, too, for the good of English cricket. I agreed, and wrote the letter, with the proviso that the selectors retained a copy of it. So obviously I had reservations and misgivings about the appointment and clearly Colin had, too, when he waited yet another week before accepting. Having taken so long to decide, I think his misgivings were such that he ought to have said 'no'. Quite obviously he didn't like the idea of serving under me, and it might have been better for both of us if he had declined to do so. However, with his acceptance of the vice-captaincy, it is probable that the whole course of cricket history was changed. If Cowdrey had declined the job – or if the selectors had consulted me, say the day after giving me the captaincy – I am sure I would have gone for Geoff Boycott as vice-captain. To my mind he was the best man technically for the job and to this day I think, technically, he is as good as anybody in the country.

The implications of what might have resulted are immense. If I had had the chance to ask for Boycott and he'd got the appointment, and if he had done a good job, he might well have been the automatic successor to me in 1973. He might never have lost the Yorkshire captaincy and I might never have gone back home as manager!

But Cowdrey accepted, and the outcome was a highly unsatisfactory relationship between captain and vice-captain, during what turned out to be a difficult and controversy-riddled tour. Nevertheless, we brought back the Ashes.

11

'SCOUNDRELS, SQUEALERS AND CHEATS'

The 1970–71 tour to Australia did not get off to the best of starts and the pessimists both at home and accompanying the tour perhaps felt their fears were well-founded when we were soundly beaten by Victoria at Melbourne. These things always look different from the sidelines and from twelve thousand miles away they may look even worse. The simple fact was that the wicket was an English-type green-top and whoever won the toss was going to put the other side in. Victoria won it and it was not exactly a surprise to us (though, of course, it was a disappointment) to be bowled out cheaply – for 142, in fact. As often happens with that type of wicket, it became progressively easier and after Victoria had declared at 304 for eight we totalled 341 in the second innings. But that still left the opposition a relatively easy target and we were beaten by six wickets. 'Outbowled, outbatted, outfielded and beaten out of sight' trumpeted the *Daily Mirror* with all the sagacity of the interested bystander. The outrageousness of such over-simplifications tend to leave one speechless.

From the start of the tour I was planning our strategy in the long term. I told both Jackie Hampshire and Don Wilson that they would not be in the side for the first two Tests because I had more or less worked out what the team was going to be. That, I believed, was the only way to play it. Unless you decide on the side and start getting it together you are going to end up with no sort of strategy at all. So I told Hampshire and Wilson: 'Enjoy yourselves but get yourselves ready – fit and in form – because if the others don't do their stuff you are going to be in after the Second Test.' The Aussies won the toss at Brisbane and batted, lost Lawry for four when the total was 12, and Stackpole was clearly run out at 18 when Boycott threw down the wicket from mid-off. The evening papers printed a picture which showed Stackpole two feet out of his ground with the bails in the air and he went on to make 207! That was the first of a series of adventures involving Stackpole on the tour and who can say what a difference a correct decision would have made to the game? What one *can* say is that there is a rather substantial difference between 18 and 207, as there is between 32 for two – which Australia should have been on the first morning – and 308 for two, their score at the end of the first day.

Nevertheless, from 372 for three, Australia crumbled to 433 all out and in fact we got a first innings lead by scoring 464. We had got right back into the game, especially after bowling them out for 214 in the second innings and then we lost a lot of time towards the end of the game (needing 184 to win), because of wet run-ups and damp patches and we ended at 39 for one. So we had come out of it well after that start, and we were not dissatisfied because we had gone into the game with an extra batsman. That is not normally my policy – I usually prefer to be carrying an extra bowler to keep control in the field, but we had been struggling a bit in our preparation and we felt we were just a bit under-prepared so we played safe. It worked out all right in the end because if it had not been for losing an hour and twenty minutes towards the end it could have been an interesting finish.

I mentioned that the decision in favour of Stackpole was the first of a series of adventures he had in the Tests because we felt there were four or five occasions when he was clearly out, only to be given not out. I am referring to incidents where he was flashing with the bat well away from the body when there could scarcely be much doubt at all about it. Perhaps the worst instance was at Sydney, where he stepped back to square slash at Derek Underwood and gave a real thick one to Alan Knott. Not out. It was really unbelievable.

I have always believed that in situations like that it is a case of the umpire making a genuine mistake. Basically one starts with the view that umpires are decent, honest men with varying degrees of experience and, consequently, varying degrees of competence. Col Eager had taken our first match against South Australia at Adelaide and, we understood, was to stand in the First Test, but then he suddenly announced his retirement. As a result we had to take the two umpires that the Australian Board nominated. So at Brisbane we had Lou Rowan and Tom Brooks, who was a hell of a nice fellow, and we had him for most of the time. At the end of the series I asked him: 'Do you mind my saying something to you, Tom?' He said, 'No', so I then told him: 'I think you've had a good series but you have erred on the side of "not out". However, you have been consistent. You've given a lot of "not outs" both ways but my view is that you have given too many.' Tom simply said, 'Thank you for telling me', and we parted the best of friends.

Having said that, let me add that we were playing under the law which made it impossible to be out lbw to a ball which pitched outside the off stump and that made it a good deal easier for an umpire to say 'not out'. We went something like twenty matches without getting an lbw decision! Now I was criticised for not bowling myself enough but consider the implications of that law – and remember that the batsmen were only too aware of what was going on. They were shuffling back and across, secure in the knowledge that they could cope with the straight-onner while they couldn't be lbw to a ball which pitched outside the leg stump or outside the off stump! I think that under those circumstances it was little short of incredible that we bowled out the Aussies at all to win the series. *We didn't have one lbw in the Test series!* If anyone requires any further explanation of my apparent reluctance to bowl myself it is simply this: I tried to concentrate on making the ball leave the right-handed batsman ... Snow, Lever, D'Oliveira and Underwood could all do that.

We went on to Perth for the Second Test and here we had an 'incident' before the game even started. I won the toss, decided to bat and went in search of the groundsman to ask for a roller. He was nowhere to be found and it was not until ten minutes or a quarter of an hour before the scheduled start that I tracked him down, only to be told that I was not allowed a roller before the start of play – it was 'his' wicket! I said, 'I think you will find you are wrong', and we went to see the umpires. One of these was Lou Rowan who told me the same thing – I wasn't allowed a roller. So we batted without a roller being used at the start of a Test match. Needless to say I was waiting for the umpires, with the Laws in my hand, when they came off at lunchtime, and both of them apologised. We got 397 and had Australia struggling at 107 for five when Ian Redpath and Greg Chappell, in his first Test, came together. Redpath got 171 and Chappell 108. They totalled 440 and on a very good wicket we declared at 287 for six. Obviously we left them a difficult target because it was a good wicket, and Tests between England and Australia have never been marked by outstanding generosity on the part of one captain to another. The match was drawn.

On the evening plane to Adelaide we discovered from a newspaper someone had brought on board that our manager (D. G. Clark, an amiable but somewhat ineffectual man) had given an interview to the Australian press in which he had said he would rather see Australia win the series than have all the Tests drawn. Not surprisingly, that didn't exactly overjoy those of us who did the actual playing! Nor was I especially pleased to be awakened at seven o'clock the following morning by 'phone calls from newspaper offices in England asking what I thought of the manager's statement. I thought it was not, perhaps, the ideal sort of remark for a manager to make.

I started off the tour with Mr Clark with a perfectly open mind. By the end of it I was forced to tell him that I honestly believed he was working more for the Australians than for us. He was, I told him, there as the team's manager, not as an ambassador of goodwill on behalf of MCC. We wanted all the help and support he could give us. However, when the Australians wanted an extra Test to be played to compensate for the rain-ruined fixture at Melbourne, we discovered that the Australian team were being paid an extra fee. Mr Clark agreed to the extra fixture without any consultation with the players, and with no mention of a match fee, so, not unreasonably, we asked, 'What about our fee? We are not contracted to play an extra match, you know.' He would not agree to a fee for the extra Test for ages, and we might even have had a mutiny: it was getting to that stage.

We had one or two 'militants' in the side, and in all honesty I had to agree that they had a valid point of view. The Aussies were getting 200 dollars a man and we were due to get nothing. It was ridiculous. We didn't want to play the extra match, in any case, because it meant playing five Tests in six weeks – and that put pressures on a touring side which were far greater than any the home team might have to experience. So we very nearly did have a mutiny.

Eventually Mr Clark agreed to ring Lord's and as soon as he spoke to Billy Griffith, the MCC secretary, he said straightaway: 'Of course you pay them a fee. Offer them £50. I'll say that now without having a meeting.' A players' meeting was held in my room and the players were already saying, 'If we don't get a match fee, we are not going to play'. Finally, the management agreed, but frankly, the amount did not delight us because the Australians were being paid substantially more. Quite honestly, the attitude seemed cheeseparing when one considered that the attendances at Tests were in the region of eighty thousand to ninety thousand a day in Melbourne; the fee seemed a piddling little amount if you took into account the loss to the Australian Board if the match was *not* played.

The whole question of the extra Test arose after the Melbourne game had been washed out on all the first four days. The pitch was a complete quagmire, although Ian Johnson (the former Test captain who had become the secretary of Victoria) kept insisting that it was fit to play and announcing to the crowd that play would begin as soon as the rain stopped. Then he went out to have a look at the ground himself and fell flat on his backside, to the undisguised delight of the whole England party! So we went on to Sydney for the Fourth Test. It is always better to play there than anywhere else in Australia, because the wickets are closer to the type we get in England. We scored 322, bowled Australia out for 236, declared at 319 for five (with Boycott 142 not out) and then Snow took seven for 40. I'll return to that performance later. It bowled Australia out for 116 and England had won the Fourth Test by 299 runs.

Then back to Melbourne we went for the Fifth, where we found the greenest wicket in Australia. This, together with a slight ridge at one end, made it the best wicket to bowl on that we had found – and the Aussies made their highest score of the series, 493 for nine declared! It moved about all over the place, bounced nastily and Basil D'Oliveira, at his pace, was hitting Bill Lawry on the hands and arms so that Peter Lever tried bowling off a Sunday League run for a bit to see if he could get the same response as Basil. But we put down two catches and got another of those decisions in favour of Stackpole. Those dropped catches may have changed the whole course of Australian cricket history, because both were offered by Ian Chappell when he was 0 and 14. Both went to Cowdrey, off, first, John Snow and then Basil D'Oliveira. At that time Chappell's Test place was very much in the balance because he had never got amongst the runs and he was really playing for his place. He went on to score 111, and was reprieved from the dropping which must inevitably have followed if either catch had been taken – and he became Australia's next captain.

Stackpole's luck with umpires moved from the astonishing to the unbelievable. He took a ball on the glove, saw it lob in a gentle parabola of a catch to Alan Knott, and set off back to the pavilion, only to find himself ruled 'not out' by a new official, Max O'Connell. On this same wicket ... still green, still bouncing ... England made 392, were then set a target of 271 in four hours to win, and declined the invitation to commit Test suicide. That is what it would have been to try to chase at that rate, because with Brian Luckhurst out with a broken finger and Dolly nursing a bruised foot we were left with three effective front-line batsmen – Boycott, Edrich and Cowdrey.

The first objective in any Test match is to win it; if that cannot be done, the next must most certainly be to avoid losing it. There was no way we could win with that sort of striking rate required, and only three fit batsmen, but we could very easily have lost by adopting a quixotic approach of appeasing the critics who were soon howling for the blood of both captains. I am all for winning; I am a hundred per cent for adopting every approach which might achieve victory. In the last innings of that Test at Melbourne there was none. We were one up in the series and it would have been something bordering on treason to have put that lead in jeopardy. Looking at the situation as a whole and taking that game in context, we had no alternative but to play it safe, to consolidate the position in the series which we had achieved. Test captains take their places in history by the mistakes they make as well as the successes they record. I had no particular desire to be remembered in the former category. Not only was there no need to take a chance; it would have been wrong to do so.

There was only one day between the end of the Fifth Test and the start of the Sixth at Adelaide but we were lucky in one respect

– normally in late January the temperature would have been round about a hundred degrees, but for some reason it stayed in the seventies for the whole five days. I can honestly say it was the best wicket I have ever seen in my life. Before its final preparation it was well-grassed and looked a bit green like an English pitch; when the game started it was white, immaculately shorn, had a perfectly uniform bounce, and to make the ball get up at all a bowler had to bang it in at his own toes. We made 470 on it after winning the toss and the Aussies started off well when Stackpole hooked Snowy's first ball for four, cut the second for four, square-cut the fourth for two and hooked the last for a four which was nearly a six.

Australia were 50 for one at close of play on the second day off 16 overs, but then were bowled out on the third for 235 at ten minutes to five. I did not enforce the follow-on and the pundits were aghast. The *Daily Mirror* thundered: '. . . the most staggering piece of thinking I can recall'. Well, I don't know exactly how much of a Test captain's thinking the *Mirror*'s Peter Laker has ever been in a position to know about, so perhaps I can tell him what mine was on that occasion.

To dispose of the Aussies we had taken the second new ball and both Snow and Lever had really let it go in the last hour of the innings. There was another hour to go as we came off the field and I said to Lever: 'How do you feel?' Pete replied, 'My shoulder is not so good but if you want to make them follow on, that's up to you'. I put the same question to Snowy who said, 'I am knackered!' Now these two had bowled for nearly an hour to get rid of the last few wickets, because Marsh, Mallett, Gleeson and Lillee all hung around for quite a bit; and what a lot of people didn't know was that in the previous Test, at Melbourne, where the humidity had been formidable, Snow had lost nearly half a stone. He doesn't shed weight easily so one had to gauge just how much this had taken out of him. I thought there was little point in throwing Snowy and 'Plank' straight back into the fray and, despite that inexplicable Aussie collapse, the wicket was still a beauty – the tail-enders had showed that. My reasoning was that Australia must have got a big score in their second innings – they weren't going to collapse twice on *that* pitch. That could have left us wanting 200-plus in our final innings on a pitch which one would reasonably have expected to be wearing a bit and turning by the last day. In addition, Gleeson was a good bowler who was bowling well. As it turned out, the pitch only started to take spin in the last two or three hours and the game was drawn. I took a bit of stick for not enforcing the follow-on; but it's very much easier to take decisions from the sidelines!

I wasn't the only one to suffer, however. Bill Lawry was sacked as captain and Ian Chappell took over. I wonder who else reflected that if Chappell had been caught at Melbourne before he had scored, he would almost certainly not even have been playing in the Seventh Test at Sydney.

Before that match, we had one more widely publicised bit of controversy to contend with. In our first innings at Adelaide Boycott was given out 'run out' when he was 58. He threw his bat down, stood with his hands on his hips, and glared at the umpire. Of course, the crowd reacted. So did the Chappell brothers, not the most sportsmanlike or gentlemanly practitioners ever to grace a cricket field. To be honest, I thought Geoff was *just* out. At Adelaide we had a perfect view, exactly sideways on like Old Trafford, and I thought his bat 'jumped' a bit just before he reached the line. It was a very, very close thing but I thought he was just out. And I believe that in his own heart of hearts Geoff thought himself that he was out, but I believe his view of it was that it was so close that he could not reasonably be *given* out. He undoubtedly had in his mind one or two of the 'not out' decisions which had been given earlier in the tour – like Stack-pole's at Brisbane – and, of course, he was intensely disappointed. But there is no excuse for behaving as he did and I felt an apology was called for. Well, when Boycs has been run out it is a waste of time anyone trying to talk to him so I left it until next day. Then I said, 'I think you should apologise to the umpire, Geoff'. He replied, 'I'll apologise – but I'll tell him I wasn't bloody out'. I told him, 'That's no sort of an apology. If that's the only way you can do it, don't bother.' He insisted, 'That's the only thing I'll say.' So I went to the umpires myself and told them: 'I am very sorry for the way Geoff behaved yesterday. If it is any help to you, *I* thought he was out. I offer the apology because I don't think that is the way to carry on.' The umpires said, 'Thanks very much; it's forgotten'. Boycs was wrong, because whether he

82

was out or not there was no excuse for throwing his bat down and acting as he did.

And so to Sydney. Before the start of the game it rained fairly solidly so the ground staff were not able to get the covers off for several days. In contrast, the outfield was lush and green and I think it was fairly obvious that whoever won the toss was going to put the opposition in. Australia won it and duly put us in. We struggled like hell, although in point of fact they didn't bowl particularly well with Lillee and Tony Dell, a left-arm opening bowler who had come into the side, spraying it about a bit. We were without Boycott who had had his left forearm broken and with Lawry now discarded, Australia, too, had a new opener in Ken Eastwood. We were bowled out for 184 and by close of play had got rid of Eastwood and Stackpole. Australia were 13 for two. That last half-hour we had at them was invaluable because if they had 'fiddled about' at the end of our innings and used up the closing stages they would have been in a very strong position on the next day.

Nevertheless, Australia got a first innings lead of 80 and with the wicket getting better as the game went on, they ought to have won. With everyone getting runs we totalled 302 in our second innings and that left the Aussies needing 223 to win. We had had to get our runs with our number one batsman, Geoff Boycott, out of the game, and we had to bowl out Australia in their second innings without our number one bowler, John Snow, who had a broken finger. No victory has ever given me so much satisfaction and it was with immense pride that I was able to say, at the end of the game: 'This has been a great team to captain. Whatever you ask of them, they produce it.' I was able to say that because, even though Snowy was able to bowl only two overs in the Aussie second innings, we still disposed of them for 160 and won by 62 runs. The Ashes were ours after twelve years. We were the first English team to win a series in Australia since Len Hutton's side, and it is not difficult to imagine how much satisfaction that gave me. We had won the series 2–0 but, sadly, we had not been able to do so without further controversy.

Australia had reached a stage in their first innings when they were just about level with our score (11 runs past us, in fact) with seven wickets down and Terry Jenner was facing Snow, who had taken the new ball about fifteen minutes earlier. Snow bowled a short-pitched delivery which was very fast, *but it wasn't a bouncer.* It was the sort of ball which, playing back, a batsman could have dealt with without undue difficulty. And remember this: Jenner had made centuries in Sheffield Shield cricket so he was no mug. As soon as he saw the ball was short, Jenner ducked, and the ball was still just a bit more than stump high when it hit Jenner on the back of the head. He had to be taken off, but I am sure that even then there need have been no trouble if Lou Rowan, as soon as everything had settled down and Snow was ready to bowl again, had not started to issue a public warning to Snowy for everyone to see.

So I went to have a word with Rowan at once, and for that I have become renowned as the England captain who waved an admonitory finger at a Test umpire. It was variously, and widely, reported that *I* had publicly given a wigging to an umpire. What no one took the trouble to find out was what my upraised finger implied. It was this: *'One bouncer. One. How can you start to issue a public warning to a bowler who has bowled just one?'* And that was presupposing that we accepted that the ball which felled Jenner was, in fact, a bouncer. It wasn't; it was a short-pitched ball.

Everyone took a photograph of that little scene with a telescopic lens. Television recorded it for posterity and everyone, it seemed, said afterwards, 'You shouldn't talk to an umpire like that'. Like what? No one took the trouble to ask if, perhaps, a different interpretation could be placed upon the incident than the one which everyone seemed to assume was the obvious one.

Certainly I asked Rowan under what law he was warning Snow and he replied, 'For persistent intimidation'. There was only one answer to that: 'There is no way under Law 46 that you can do that when he has bowled *one* short ball.' Rowan then walked over and tried to get Tom Brooks on his side and Brooks said he didn't want anything to do with it – he thought there was nothing wrong. But Rowan still took it upon his own head to give Snowy an official warning. John, by this time, was a bit explosive (which I regarded as perfectly understandable) and what worried me, knowing Snowy's temperament, was that he was quite likely to go and bowl two real bouncers on the trot. I would then have been without my main bowler! So that is why I made my point to Rowan at some length. Mercifully, we got to the end of the over without further incident, and Snow then went down to fine leg where a few cans and bottles startled whistling around his ears, so I shouted him back up to the middle.

Now this is where no one, not even Jim Swanton, will have it that what we did was justified. We all sat down in the middle while the police cleared off the thirty or forty cans and bottles which had been thrown. Then I said, 'Right, we'll start again now'. Snow walked back to fine leg, a spectator came over the fence and grabbed him and the bottles started to shower on to the field once again. Now this was not the first opportunity the authorities and the police had had to stop all the nonsense; it was the second. If Rowan had been half as concerned about law and order as he had been in an incomparably less explosive situation at Brisbane, then it all could have been sorted out with a minimum of bother. In the First Test, a youth had been sitting on the fence at Brisbane and Rowan had walked sixty or seventy yards down the edge to tell him to tuck his legs over the other side. At Sydney the same umpire now did nothing at all when I can guarantee that there were something like a hundred and fifty cans and bottles whistling past a player's head. By this time, frankly I was livid.

There is no argument about it. The umpires should have stopped the game at that point. There is absolutely no way you can play a game of cricket, even at deep fine leg, with bottles and cans whistling about your head.

The umpires did nothing, so as far as I am concerned I was absolutely and totally justified in saying to the players, 'Right, we'll go off the field until they have sorted this lot out'. I was certainly not going to have one of my players standing, a stationary target, while idiots threw cans and bottles at him. So off we went.

We went to the dressing-room, and there I found that the manager did not agree with my decision. I had a few choice words with David Clark on the matter. His attitude was: 'Get back on the field – you've got to get back out there.' My attitude was equally simple but not exactly on the same lines. 'If you want to go out there, manager, and get your head knocked off, you *can* do. Until we get it sorted out, and an apology over the loud-speaker system, we are not going back on.' Then Snowy joined

85

in and got rather a lot off his chest. The manager, in fact, had to side-step a bit; Snowy in that mood is rather a lively customer!

Eventually Lou Rowan came in with Alan Barnes, the Sydney Cricket Ground secretary, and I told him: 'Get on that microphone and tell the crowd that there has got to be no more trouble. If you get that sorted out, then we'll go back out there.' Barnes didn't want to make an announcement. He could see nothing wrong – that made him a great secretary, didn't it? And then Rowan joined in: 'If you don't come back on the field you'll have to forfeit the game.' I replied: 'We'll come back providing it is made perfectly clear to the crowd that there must be no more bottle-throwing. We are simply not going to stand out there as Aunt Sallys, and if there is any more bottle-throwing we come straight off whether we lose the Test match or not.' And I told the manager the same. In the end we went back and there was no more trouble. I am glad to say that through the whole of the furore the team were behind me. We were very much *a team*, and there was no trouble on that score. The British press and commentators were, I think, rather divided, but what pleased me most of all was that there were four former Australian Test captains in the press box and every one of them wrote that I was perfectly justified in my course of action. They said they were ashamed of the crowd behaviour and that it could not be allowed to continue.

Afterwards I got literally hundreds of letters from Australians and for every one that 'knocked' I'll bet there were a hundred which said they were ashamed of the crowd's behaviour, and that we did the right thing in coming off.

Perhaps the most colourful defence came in an article by a well-known Australian columnist called Ron Saw, couched in the sort of extravagant phraseology which is a hallmark of Australian journalism. He wrote:

'Normally I adopt a healthy, uncomplicated, red-blooded Australian attitude to English cricketers. I regard them as scoundrels, squealers and cheats – and the more soundly they thrash us the ruddier runs my blood.

'But I'll turn blue before I blame Ray Illingworth for leading his team off the Sydney Cricket Ground. I have nothing but admiration for a captain who'll stick up for his players, who'll stand up to nagging umpires and howling slobs and to my mind Illingworth on Saturday showed more guts and more common-sense than has been shown by anyone in this entire series.

'A few more Illingworths and fewer canting Pollyannas – both press and public – and cricket might become a game of spirit instead of a bureaucrat-burdened bore. As long as cricket is played people will argue about the walk-off, looking for some-one to blame.

'John Snow is copping it. So are the drunks on The Hill. The English press has tipped the bucket over Illingworth. For my two centsworth I'll take the umpire. If he'd shown more tact nothing at all would have happened.

'Consider the facts: John Snow made a ball rise sharply. Terry Jenner, who isn't a bad bat, got in the way, was felled and carried off. And Lou Rowan, rather too emotionally, warned Snow. The umpire should have known better. He should have known there would be an uproar from The Hill. Someone or other wrote that "the mob was in an ugly mood". What a puny euphemism! The mob on The Hill was drunk. Smashed. Orry-eyed. All day long in the heat and humidity they'd been pouring the stuff into themselves. That's neither condemnation nor excuse. The fact is that there were more howling, dangerous drunks on The Hill than I've seen before and it was madness to stir them up with what was, after all, a marginal decision. Marginal? Of course it was marginal. Snow hadn't been intimidating Jenner. He was warned, impulsively, because Jenner had been hurt. It's fair to say that he was warned not for bowling bumpers at Jenner but for bowling bumpers through the series. Australia's bowlers had been flinging them around, too, but the Australian bumpers had been garbage and Snow's had been dynamite.

'Snow blew his temper and so did Illingworth ... and if a captain wants to lose his temper in defence of his team, if he wants to behave like a human being instead of a stuffed mullet, he'll get my vote every time.'

Stirring, picturesque stuff. But it says most of what needed to be said and from an Australian who makes his standpoint ex-tremely clear in his opening paragraph, more than welcome. I wish some of our own correspondents could have seen the situation as clearly.

Looking back at some of the personalities of the tour, I had to stick my neck out a bit to get Basil D'Oliveira in the party. I think Cowdrey must have had a bit of trouble with him in the West Indies and there was a faction which was a bit anti-Dolly. I told him what the situation was and stressed, 'Don't you let me down'. He went through the tour, never put a foot wrong and did everything I asked of him. He has a great temperament, doesn't mind how long he has to wait to go in (and not every batsman is good in this respect) and he was a great help to everyone on the tour.

On the field he could always swing it a bit – not easy in Australia – and he could always bowl to a slip or two. Boycott, Edrich and Luckhurst all had a good series and Dolly made some useful scores in the middle order with Alan Knott and myself. The tail made runs from time to time which were more than useful to us and Snow bowled as well as any fast bowler I have ever seen. I have played with a lot – Trueman, Statham, Willis, and the rest, and I don't think any of them could have bowled better than Snowy did. He got a little bit tired towards the end of the tour, especially after losing that half-stone in Melbourne, but having said that, I don't think any batsman in the world could have played John with that new ball. He had a superb tour. He got chest-high bounce from only just short of a length, he got movement off the pitch but above all he bowled a beautiful line: fractionally outside the off stump, so that if the ball did even just a little bit he had every batsman in trouble. Snow was magnificent. I have never seen a fast bowler bowl better.

He looked after himself, too; he was always fit ... never got 'popped up' like many tourists are tempted to do, and in almost every way he was an excellent tourist. His only fault – and after all he did, it was difficult to complain about it – was that it didn't mean much to him if a tail-ender came in and whacked him back over his head. That meant runs which could be important to the outcome, but Snowy never looked at it like that. He hadn't the competitiveness of, say, F.S., who would go mad if a tail-end batsman hit him anywhere, let alone over his head.

We hadn't any real problem players. Cowdrey wasn't a problem in the sense of not being fit or 'playing out'. He had been on several tours before and he tended to go off with his own friends. We rarely saw him. In a way, his lack of team spirit was a bit of a let-down. After all, he was my vice-captain.

It was a pity. This was a throw-back to the 1962–63 tour and, frankly, I think that if you are still having problems after all that time you shouldn't take the job. Right from the start at Adelaide Colin made it clear he was not really interested. He missed nets one day without a word to me or the manager and that, in a vice-captain, is not very good. He had a bad tour ... he didn't make runs, and even his normally excellent slip fielding let him down – so much so that in the end I had to take him out of the slips. Once you have done that there are not many places in the field to put Colin; he couldn't do much chasing on those big Australian grounds!

We had a certain amount of misfortune with our bowlers. Alan Ward had to be flown home and then Ken Shuttleworth injured himself and was never the same man who took five for 40 at Brisbane. But Bob Willis came out as a very young replacement for Wardie and did a great job. He had to learn a lot and some of it was not easy. For instance we had to tell him that while keeping the same line he had to bowl about a yard further up to Stackpole, who was such a good back-foot player, than he had to, say, Greg Chappell. He listened, he learned, he did his stuff and he got us a wicket almost every time he went on to bowl. Pete Lever has a great big heart and he gave us absolutely everything he had got. I'm sure he went back a forty per cent better bowler than he went out.

'Plank' had almost always to bowl uphill or into the wind because Snowy, of course, was the senior bowler and Lever did it all with the utmost goodwill and good humour. One day I bowled him down a slope and he said he nearly fell flat on his face. Now the simple ability to laugh at that sort of situation, to be able to make light of what is, after all, solid graft and grinding effort is worth so much to a captain.

Derek Underwood, too, bowled splendidly, especially when we were trying to keep things tight. He bowled with marvellous control, got us the odd wicket and then we were able to throw Snowy back in again.

It was in many ways a controversial tour. There were moments I am glad I shan't have again. But we brought back the Ashes. We beat Australia *in* Australia. We did it with a team which was very much a team in every sense of the word. We did it in spite of a lot of problems which we could well have done without ... but we did it and I shall always be very, very proud of that.

*   *   *   *   *

To move on to New Zealand after a full tour of Australia was always an anti-climax, so it is a good thing for cricket generally that the New Zealanders now get a visiting tour in their own right, even though it involves only three Tests. On England's visit in 1978 Ken Barrington, manager of the side, said at a dinner in Auckland that he felt the time was fast approaching for New Zealand to have a full five-Test tour. That is something I am sure cricketers of every country would welcome.

The old system was unfair to everyone. To go to that lovely country after an exhausting tour of Australia meant that players arrived physically and psychologically drained. That point cannot be over-emphasised. A Test series in Australia is cricket at its highest level, and at its most intense. Every day of every Test leaves you feeling as though you have been in a particularly strenuous battle. It demands total concentration for every minute of the game and after five days of that you simply want to get away from it all and think about something entirely different – or sometimes simply to think about nothing at all. Instead, you are whipped away up-country to utterly meaningless one-day games which amount to nothing more than a Roman holiday for a crowd who have often travelled a hundred miles or more for six hours of undignified slog. Yet these people, not least because they *have* travelled so far, are fully entitled to their only glimpse of the touring side in action and the only chance they get in a year or more to see first-class cricketers play. No tourist begrudges them their one day of fun and frolic. But every tourist at one time or another has wished that that was his match to be off duty so that he could lounge on Bondi Beach or amble round a golf course at his own pace.

The games, and the travel involved, mean that physical exhaustion is added to one's mental fatigue, with the result that every player arrives in New Zealand feeling that the last thing he wants to see is a cricket ground. It's unfair to touring players, and their attitude is in turn unfair to the players of the host country and thus to the public.

I discussed all this at length with the New Zealand officials, and my own view was that it would be better to *start* a tour down under by going to New Zealand first, where we could regard the matches as a full-scale warm-up for those in Australia. Certainly it would be better preparation to play three Tests there first than the preparation a tour party gets after arriving in Australia. The snag, from a New Zealand point of view, was the difficulty in getting the grounds ready for Test cricket by early November. Eden Park, in Auckland, Lancaster Park, at Christchurch, and Carisbrooke, Dunedin, are all first and foremost rugby grounds, while soccer is played on the Basin Reserve, Wellington. It often seems little short of a miracle that they can be made ready for Test cricket by February, let alone November, so that is, of course, a major stumbling block. One alternative I thought about was for England to visit New Zealand in the middle of the Australian tour, cutting out some of those up-country games – but I don't suppose that would meet with general approval in Australia.

So it is good to see New Zealand now with its own short series – Pakistan, in 1979, following England there in 1978 – because it is a country most Englishmen (perhaps I should say Britons) thoroughly enjoy visiting. It is so much more like the British Isles than any other part of the Commonwealth – naturally beautiful on a scale which is breathtaking in most areas. The people, whose hospitality is legendary, are extremely British in their outlook. That is meant as an Englishman's compliment and I hope no Kiwi will construe it as patronising. I would like to see tours to New Zealand where our team could be fresh and interested in their game and where they could really enjoy their cricket on grounds like Nelson and New Plymouth and Hamilton as well as the less attractive rugby-cum-cricket stadia in the bigger centres of population. The Test grounds are not great, certainly not as Test match grounds. I like Christchurch immensely as a city, for instance, but Lancaster Park provided us with the biggest slow turner of all time ... not the best pitch on which to play a Test match as 'Deadly' Underwood proved to them. The Number Six Section at Lancaster Park has the reputation of housing the most vociferous spectators in the country, at cricket as well as rugby, but – I'm sorry to disappoint them! – to us they sounded a completely civilised crowd after those in Australia. When you have been in Aussie for five months, the worst that Number Six Section could provide would always sound like a vicarage garden party.

Aussies are a breed all of their own. I have some good friends there, like all Englishmen, but as a race they are brash in the extreme. As long as you talk to them in their own language, you'll get by: we used to tell them they were like their country – big and empty. That sort of language they can understand, but I imagine that anyone who was of a particularly refined and delicate nature would find them a bit of a handful. They love to boast, for instance, and in Sydney one of the things they have always liked to boast about most of all is their Harbour Bridge. On the 1962–63 tour, Fred Trueman was at a cocktail party where a group of Aussies were going on about it quite a bit. F.S. listened until he had had enough, then slowly put down his glass and addressed the assembled Australians: 'Bloody famous landmark?' he snarled. 'Bloody famous *Australian* landmark? Let me tell you, me old flower, it was copied from the Tyne Bridge in Newcastle, built by a Yorkshire firm, Dorman Long, and what's more you haven't paid for the bugger yet!' It is not easy to silence Australians but Fred managed it.

In a way, I suppose, Australians are a bit like Yorkshire people – not entirely reticent when it comes to speaking their minds. Certainly their crowds loved Fred and the more he abused them the more they seemed to love him for it. Most English players have returned from Australia with particular memories of the brutally frank wit of spectators, especially, of course, The Hill in Sydney and it is usually with some tale to tell against themselves. Peter Parfitt's undying memory is of the anguish of one stentorian spectator, watching a Parfitt rearguard action, who roared: 'Parfitt – I wish you was a statue and I was a bloody seagull!' And Neil Hawke particularly likes the advice offered, treble *fortissimo*, to Alan Davidson who, bowling to the Reverend David Shepherd, delivered an over so uncharacteristically wide that the future Bishop of Liverpool did not have to play a single stroke. 'Caam awn, Dyvo', came the biblical exhortation from The Hill, 'lead him into temptyshun'.

Brash the Australian may be, but is there a cricket spectator anywhere in the world with a sharper or more caustic wit?

New Zealanders, by comparison, are diffident in the extreme with the isolated exceptions of that particular section in Christchurch, and 'Cans Corner' at Auckland, a name derived from the quite astonishing number of empty beer cans which are to be found there at the end of a day's play. But unlike Sydney's Hill, the regulars of Cans Corner store their empties neatly in sacks so that they can be carted conveniently away each evening. That, perhaps as well as anything else, points the difference between Australian and New Zealand spectators – the difference between non-discipline and self-discipline.

Comments from Cans Corner are frequent, raucous, and very much to the point. Usually they are channelled through the impressive vocal chords of one Ian Donnelly, a great character with a tremendous sense of humour, who really knows and loves his cricket. During the Third Test against England, in March, 1978, he was in rather good voice and as his pitch was next door to the radio and television commentary boxes, listeners and viewers got a close-up rendering of his sallies throughout the game. One listener who had had enough after three days sent Ian a telegram, care of the radio commentary box, which was duly delivered and which, to his great delight, read: 'Suggest voice-transplant with a drunken parrot.'

12

BIG BAD JOHN AND LITTLE SUNNY

Back in England for the 1971 season, the visit of India and Pakistan promised something of a respite from both the playing problems and the controversy of Australia – but even that was not to be. In the First Test at Lord's, Sunil Gavaskar, the little Indian opening batsman who was destined to become one of their greatest of all time, was knocked to the ground by John Snow, following through, as the batsmen tried to scamper a quick single. Snow, at that precise moment, was no doubt steaming with exasperation as all genuinely fast bowlers are at many moments in their careers. But within seconds the utterly ludicrous aspect of the situation had taken over – on the field, at least. Big Bad John and Little 'Sonny'. It was just too daft for words for anyone to look upon it as a physical attack by one player on another. Snowy took a lot of good-natured stick about 'picking on someone his own size', and in the normal course of a Test match evening he and Gavaskar were in the middle of a group of players with the light-hearted back-chat still going on.

But we all reckoned without the reaction of officialdom. This was at Lord's, and Snow was *ordered* to apologise by Billy Griffith, then secretary of the TCCB. The whole episode was a *cause célèbre* in the media for some days, certainly for long after the players had forgotten it – with the possible exception of John Snow himself, who was dropped for the Second Test and smouldered with resentment for a long time afterwards. My own view was that there was a good deal of over-reaction by just about everyone except Gavaskar.

The Test itself (in case anyone has forgotten, a match really was being played) was drawn and so was the Second at Old Trafford, where I had the satisfaction of getting my second Test century and where rain washed out the last day with us in an impregnable position. So it was a bit of a shock to lose at The Oval, giving India their first Test win ever on English soil, and with it the rubber, after they had trailed by 71 on the first innings. I had bowled 34 overs for 70 runs and five wickets so clearly the Indian spinners were looking at the pitch with some interest and, sure enough, Chandrasekhar bowled us out for 101, leaving the tourists to make 173 – and to make history. They did it with a good deal of grim determination (and I am certainly not one to condemn them for that) and a bit of characteristic sparkle from Farokh Engineer. *Wisden* reported: 'Tension was high and the Indians, avoiding all risks, took three hours to make the last 97 runs. Illingworth, in his own way, again bowled beautifully but without luck; and his field-placings were masterly, as was his handling of the attack.' Maybe ... but we lost.

Intikhab's Pakistanis followed in the second half of what was a poor summer for cricket weather, and though we drew two Tests we won the other and now we had to await the arrival of Ian Chappell's Australians in pursuit of those Ashes. Two Tests were won by each side and one was drawn in a series which began on my fortieth birthday. After a very wet spring there was a lot of moisture around when I won the toss at Old Trafford, and after a lot of thought I decided to bat. We weren't terribly impressive, apart from Tony Greig, playing in his first Test, and John Edrich, who played exactly the sort of grafting innings one expected of him when the going was difficult. The Aussies never recovered after being shot out for 142 without a single ball being spun in anger, and despite the weather (perhaps because of it to some extent) we won by 89 runs – only to find the positions reversed on going to Lord's.

Dennis Lillee – a man whose bowling I had already experienced on a pitch like polished glass at Perth – had arrived on the scene, but while he looked a fine bowler at Lord's he took only four wickets. Our problems there were created by a gentleman called Bob Massie. History records that Massie played only six Tests in his life but neither he, nor we, will forget Lord's, 1972, in a hurry. He took 16 wickets for 137, and by the fourth day we had lost by eight wickets.

The Third Test at Trent Bridge was drawn and the Fourth, at

Headingley, had been under way for less than two hours before we had complaints about the pitch from Australia. Certainly it was unusual, to say the least, to find myself bowling in harness with Underwood before lunch on the first day, but any suggestion that the wicket had been 'doctored' to suit us is absolute nonsense. It is true that it was the sort of pitch to which English batsmen are very much more accustomed than the Australians are, and it posed problems of technique which were certainly searching ones for the Aussies. It was a grafter's pitch, on which you had to be prepared to work for your runs; there was not much of a price for the exotic stroke-maker. It was the sort of pitch on which Herbert Sutcliffe played in masterly fashion, on which Len Hutton showed his class, on which Geoff Boycott has played outstandingly well. It was a pitch on which I was prepared to graft for four-and-a-half hours for 57. And it was the sort of pitch on which Underwood has, for many years, been the best bowler in the world. We won by 10 wickets and 'Deadly' took 10 wickets in the match for 82.

A splendid series was squared by Australia at The Oval, where both Chappell brothers scored centuries in the first innings and Lillee had 10 wickets in the match. Thus England retained the Ashes, but certainly not without a struggle. Packerism was in the future, and this was an Australian side full of talent and full of fight.

At the end of the season I needed a rest. At forty, the thought of an eight-Test tour of Pakistan and India was not particularly inviting, much as I would have enjoyed bowling on Indian wickets. The main part of India's attack has been spin for so long that I have often wanted to find out for myself what different aspects of technique are required on their grassless pitches. I would have enjoyed the cricket. But I was tired, and I was keen to see something of my family with two daughters now growing up. To be perfectly frank, in considering as well that my stomach has never been terribly enthusiastic about infusions of Oriental spices, I reflected that I could make twice as much money in my winter job at home as I would get for slogging through Nagpur and Kanpur, Hyderabad (Pakistan) to Hyderabad (India). I declined the invitation to tour, and Tony Lewis led England in eight Tests. All three in Pakistan were drawn and in India they won one, lost two and drew two.

At the start of the 1973 season, with New Zealand and West Indies as the tourists, the selectors perpetrated one of those pieces of nonsense which seem to have bedevilled Test cricket since the game began. We had to have a Test trial with Tony Lewis and myself as rival captains. Now this to me was ludicrous. I had skippered England with reasonable success over four seasons and an overseas tour, and I assumed there was not much left for the selectors to learn about my ability both as a captain and as a player. Tony had been in university and county cricket since 1955, and had led two tours abroad as well as skippering Glamorgan since 1967. What more did they need to know about him? If he, on his record (and having accepted the tour I had declined) had been appointed captain at the start of 1973, I don't suppose I would have had particularly strong grounds for complaint.

If, on the other hand, the selectors had said, 'Illy's got a fair record over the last few years. We know his capabilities and Lewis has not done enough yet as captain to supersede him', then maybe Tony might have felt *he* had no complaint. I don't know. But to pit us against each other ... what were they trying to prove, or what were they seeking to learn, that they didn't already know? It seemed stupid to me.

As things turned out, Tony got a first-baller (which might have been what cost him the captaincy) and I put on over a hundred with Frank Hayes when we were in trouble against Geoff Arnold on a green 'un. Tony skippered the team which had been in India, I captained 'The Rest' in a close game which depended on declarations – and we just managed to win. I don't think it proved anything at all, but I got the job against New Zealand. I had had a fairly good match, while everything went wrong for Tony, but I don't think that proved anything one way or the other. It seemed ludicrous for one to have to put oneself 'on the line' in that way. I had accepted, when I declined to tour India, that Tony Lewis might be made captain when he came back and I'm sure he had his hopes. If the selectors had thought he was the better man for the job, they should have made him captain straightaway instead of subjecting both of us to the elaborate charade of a trial.

Anyway, Lewis became my vice-captain which was right because presumably, having decided it was such a close thing between us, the selectors were thinking in terms of grooming him as my successor. So what happened? He played one Test against the New Zealanders and then disappeared from the Test scene, initially because of a leg injury, but never to return. And when *I* got the chop at the end of that summer the selectors found themselves in the position of giving the England captaincy to a man who, according to cricket's grapevine, was on the verge of losing the captaincy of his own county! But that's another story. What Tony Lewis thought about the events of that 1973 summer, I don't know. But if I ever hear him musing during Test match commentary on the strange whims of selectors I shall have a certain amount of sympathy.

13

POLITICS OMNIA VINCIT?

The West Indies tour to England in 1973 saw the end of my career as a Test captain which was a tremendous disappointment to me. One always knows that it has got to end sometime but, ideally, one would like to be in a position to say, 'Well, I've done my job and I think I have done it reasonably well. Now it's time for me to stand down and let a new and younger captain take over.' Certainly that is how I would have liked to bow out, rather than being deposed after a series which I genuinely felt could so easily have turned out very differently.

The West Indies were always going to be formidable opposition, because virtually all the party were stars in their own right in the English county championship: for example, Sobers, Kanhai, Fredericks, and Lloyd. We were also going to have Keith Boyce coming in at number nine and we were going to face an exceptionally strong fast bowling side, too. They were not particularly strong in spin-bowling but they had Lance Gibbs and he was not exactly the world's worst. Additionally, they all had experience, lots of experience, of playing in English conditions; so in many ways it was going to be a 'home' series for them. Even so, I think if we had played them on slow turners we might well have beaten them. As it was, all three wickets had a touch of green and consequently a bit of pace. Even so, the First Test at The Oval was not a bad match and if we had had just the odd rub of the green we might have won it. Our lads bowled well on the first day, beat the bat a good deal but didn't get that touch of luck that every side needs. There wasn't much in it at the end. At Edgbaston, if we had held our catches, we would have won. In their second innings Gary Sobers came in, played forward to me and gave Frank Hayes, at slip, the easiest catch you have ever seen.

It just curled lazily to him . . . so slowly, in fact, that Frank closed his hands on it before the ball had arrived and it hit him on the outside of the hand and went down. Frank said afterwards: 'Look, there's nothing I can say. It is just one of those things which will never happen again.' Fair enough. It has happened to all of us. But you don't usually put down G. St Aubyn Sobers in a Test match without paying rather heavily for it. An over or so later Clive Lloyd went to sweep me, got a top edge and was dropped by Geoff Arnold at deep square leg.

Like Gary, Big Hubert isn't a batsman it is advisable to let off the hook. If we had held those two catches I think we would have won, and thus gone to Lord's with the series all square. As it turned out, the match was drawn and so we were in the final Test one down. It was a good wicket which got a shade faster as the game went on, but we had gone into it with the wrong side. The idea was that Tony Greig was going to be rested because he was about a stone-and-a-half under weight and a bit shattered; but when we got to Lord's Chris Old announced that his ankle was bothering him, so we had to go into the game with a pace attack consisting of Bob Willis, Geoff Arnold and Greggy, a very tired and unfit Greggy. Bob Willis bowled magnificently – and very quick. Arnold set off at the other end and after one or two overs I said to him, 'What's the matter with you?' He replied, 'I don't know . . . I don't feel to have anything left in me at all'. That was great news for me, on the first day of a vital Test on a good wicket, and against a batting line-up like the one the West Indies presented to us!

I was furious. 'For God's sake', I demanded, 'why didn't you say something before we started? It's no use coming into a Test match, then running up and saying you have nothing left.' So I had to put Greig on and, as I've said, he was shattered and went for 30-odd in his first six overs. I was left on a belting wicket with one quickie. Bob Willis was tremendous. He kept going at full pace against one of the finest line-ups of batsmen in the world with no help at the other end. If he had had any help it is conceivable that we might have controlled them to a 300 score; instead they totalled over 600, and we were out of the game before we had started. It was unfortunate, then, that we didn't bat very well. It's never easy when you have been out in the field for more than two days but even allowing for that we still didn't bat well and they bowled us out twice. The pitch was fast and the bounce was uneven and the West Indian quicks, firing on all cylinders, banged it in and left us to worry about what the ball was going to do. It was the occasion, too, when Geoff Boycott fell for the sucker punch – the Windies dropping it short and more or less defying him to hook them. Of course, he holed out, and there was a great bust-up in the pavilion at close of play.

I pitched into Boycott because I had to, but not just because he had got out hooking right at the end of the day. Apparently Brian Luckhurst had said to him, 'Do you mind taking the last over?' and Geoff had agreed. Then he was furious with himself for getting out – for falling into a very obvious trap, in fact. When he came into the dressing-room he started sounding off at Lucky and I told him: 'Just shut up, Geoff. I know you are fed up and a bit strung up about getting out but leave it for the time being.' But no. He came back and started all over again. Well, I just couldn't have that so I came down on him like a ton of bricks. 'Shut your mouth', I said, 'or I'll shut it for you'.

That night he went to hospital with a nose-bleed and the story went around that I had bopped him one. I'm glad to say that it didn't come to that but I think the story has stuck, just the same. Geoff does get nose-bleeds when pressure builds up around him and, in fact, it happened again during the same match. When it was announced that I hadn't got the captaincy for the tour that winter, I rang Boycs up to tell him that Mike Denness had been made captain. And he had a nose-bleed that night too!

Playing that Test had been rather like fighting a battle with half the army wounded and the other half playing a *kamikaze* role. I didn't, however, feel in all honesty that the performance was a typical example of the way England teams had normally played under my captaincy. My departure, I'm quite sure, was political, but I have never been able to ferret out the real truth of what happened. One source, close to one of the selectors, told me that two selectors were asked to leave the room while the name of the captain to tour the West Indies was chosen. From another source, well-known to me personally, came a denial of that suggestion. What I *do* know is that in the morning, I had been ninety-nine per cent certain to get the job; when the decision was made, in the afternoon of the same day, I didn't get it. Now it can't have been anything which happened on the field during that brief period which changed the minds of the selectors. It had to be a political move and, from what I have been able to sort out, it almost certainly involved intervention by someone outside the selection committee.

The West Indies innings had lasted most of the first two days; we were halfway through our innings when the captain was picked, so no one knew which way the game was going to go (except, of course, that we weren't going to win it). So what did happen behind the scenes at Lord's between the start of play and the tea interval that day? I would dearly love to know. The only clue I have ever been able to pick up is that a certain Very Important Person in the Lord's hierarchy had expressed the view that I was 'getting too much say in what happened'. If that is the truth of the matter, then it is almost as laughable as it is infuriating – because for something like thirty years that venerable gentleman has interfered in, and wielded influence over, matters which should never be his concern at all. We may never know just how profound and far-reaching that influence has been, but that it has existed for so long there can be no doubt.

14

THE BREAK WITH YORKSHIRE

In June, 1968, I was thirty-six years old. I had been a professional cricketer for seventeen years, and while I had no particular reason for believing my career was reaching its end I had, realistically, to tell myself that it was certainly more than halfway over. With a wife and two small daughters, I had to start thinking seriously about my future. A sporting career of any kind is, by its very nature, insecure to some extent and, when I thought about the years ahead when I had finished playing cricket, I needed some kind of assurance.

I knew I was good for three years or more in top-class cricket, so I asked Yorkshire to give me a three-year contract. They would not be risking anything by doing so, I felt. Even if I lost form after a couple of those years I had enough experience to be useful to them as a coach, and to pass on something of what I had learned over seventeen years in a very hard and expert school. I didn't expect to lose form; indeed, I didn't expect to be any less of a player in three years time. But looking at everything from the club's, as well as my own point of view, I felt my request for guaranteed security for the next three years was not unreasonable. There was no precedent for this. Indeed, Yorkshire's policy was to contract players annually. But simply because a system had operated over a long period didn't seem to me to be a valid reason for continuing to operate it for evermore. Players in the pre-war era had a good deal more security than we had in 1968, for the simple reason that they were well paid in relation to the average working man's earnings. You could save a bit of money out of a county cricketer's wage in the 1930s; you could in the first five or six years after the war. Then average earnings started to outstrip a cricketer's pay, and it never caught up again. So my request to the committee did not seem unreasonable, let alone revolutionary.

Sadly, there was a school of thought in high Yorkshire cricket places which regarded my proposal as revolutionary in the extreme. I have never had the opportunity to make my point of view clear, so let me do it now; because Brian Sellers, who really ruled cricket in my county for so long, put it about during my absence on tour in Australia – at a special general meeting when Brian Close had been relieved of the captaincy – that I had left because I wanted more money. *That is absolutely untrue.* I was, in fact, a firm believer in the principle that all capped players should be paid the same wage.

Brian Close and Fred Trueman believed otherwise, and we often had arguments about this – sensible, sane arguments, but our views were entirely different. My point was that when I first went into the Yorkshire side I was paid (on being capped) the same as Len Hutton, who was the greatest batsman in the world at that time. Similarly, young players now came in without one-tenth of Brian's or Fred's or my experience, and they were paid the same as us. In short, it evened itself out over the years, and it was by far the best thing for team spirit to have all capped players on the same amount. So my approach to the committee was not about money; it was about security. I had finished the previous season as the leading wicket-taker in the country, so, as I have said, I did not think I was asking the committee to take an undue risk even if I was asking them to break with tradition.

First I put my point to John Nash, the Yorkshire secretary, and he said he felt I was rather like Wilfred Rhodes and could go on playing until I was fifty! Consequently it seemed to me a little inconsistent when the committee declined to offer me a contract which would have taken me up to the age of only thirty-nine. However, Mr Nash subsequently told me that the county were not willing to offer a contract and I told him: 'In that case I am afraid I shall have to hand in my resignation.' I was asked to put it in writing, which I did. I handed the letter to Mr Nash at a game at Park Avenue. In the normal course of events, the letter would then have gone before the committee; but before that could happen, Mr Nash rang Brian Sellers who offered what might be described as a characteristic comment: I could go, and any other bugger who wanted to go could go with me.

THE BREAK WITH YORKSHIRE

Now I did not want any of this made public before it had all
been officially sorted out, and I asked Freddie Trueman (a
columnist for *The People* on Sundays) not to publish the story
at that stage. So I was rather surprised to be approached by Bill
Bowes (the former Yorkshire bowler who was then writing cricket
for the *Yorkshire Evening Post*). I asked who had told him about
the possibility of my leaving Yorkshire, and he said, 'Mr Nash
has asked me to handle it on behalf of the press'. 'But', I told
him, 'my letter has only gone in today. It can't have been seen
by the committee.' 'Oh', replied Bill, 'Brian Sellers has said you
can go and any other bugger with you.' So the King was ruling
with his absolute authority once again. I am convinced that if
my letter had been considered by the committee, soberly and
sensibly, before the matter was publicised as a *fait accompli*, I
might never have left Yorkshire.

There were obviously members of the committee who did not
and would not want me to leave Yorkshire. In my heart of hearts
I didn't want to leave. But since the committee were never given
a chance to consider the position and I can be just as stubborn
as Brian Sellers, I went. However, I am nothing if not practical.
In considering my position, I had never contemplated leaving my
work without having a suitable alternative. With a wife and family
you don't simply walk out and join the ranks of the unemployed.
In case the worst came to the worst and I had to make good
my threat to resign, I had been looking around and I knew that
one or two jobs were available to me, including professional positions in the Leagues. I went to see all the counties who were
interested ... Nottinghamshire, Northamptonshire, Leicestershire ... there were one or two others as well. The best paid of
these jobs was going to be at Nottinghamshire, but that did not
include the captaincy. In my last season or two at Yorkshire I
had begun to fancy the idea of skippering a side myself, and now
seemed the best opportunity. Northamptonshire were probably
the second best in financial terms, with Leicestershire and Lancashire about on a par but there was only a hundred or two in
difference between them all after Nottinghamshire. I didn't fancy
going as far south as Sussex, who were also interested; while
Lancashire has just appointed Jackie Bond as captain.

I wanted security for a few years; I wanted to go somewhere

where I thought I would be able to enjoy my cricket in my last few years in the game, and I wanted to go to a county where I thought there was a chance I might do some good and get a decent side together. I couldn't be captain at Nottinghamshire, as I said; Northants did in fact offer me the captaincy after the imminent retirement of Roger Prideaux, but Leicestershire offered me the job straightaway. Even so, there is no way they would have got me there but for one seemingly irrelevant factor – they had recently completed new dressing-room accommodation. I had spent years walking apprehensively down two flights of rickety stairs, collecting splinters in my feet on the way to take a shower, and I absolutely would not have contemplated doing that again in every home game! But Leicestershire had built this new accommodation, Mike Turner was clearly an ambitious young secretary, and the club seemed as though it was keen to go places. All in all there seemed a better chance of my doing something there than with most of the others.

Leicestershire certainly seemed to have the greatest potential. The first thing I had to do was to get rid of a built-in acceptance of defeat. Now that takes a lot of doing, especially when a club has never won anything. For years they had been a chopping-block for almost everyone else; for instance, Yorkshire in their heyday used to book in for only two nights when playing there, and these things become deeply ingrained in a side's mental outlook. So I felt we were going to need an infusion of new players, five or six of them, not simply to increase the collective ability of the side but because I needed men who were not conditioned to accept defeat, men into whom I could instil something of my own confidence and a more positive approach to the game. There were some players of ability and experience there ... Maurice Hallam, Peter Marner, Clive Inman ... but within a year or so they left the county. To be honest, I was in agreement with this because, probably, they had become a little too fixed in their ideas.

So by the time I had been there for three years we had acquired about eight new players, many of them young, which dramatically improved our fielding – and that had to be number one priority. If you have only moderately good bowlers, an outstanding fielding side can make them so much better and can give the captain control in the field. Roger Tolchard was there, John

Steele came along, Paul Haywood and Geoff Tolchard were fine fielders. Graeme McKenzie joined at the same time as me; then a few years later Ken Higgs arrived, giving us two opening bowlers with a lot of experience. Provided that we fielded well, we were going to be a useful side when we were attacking. This helped us, first, to get a little bit on the winning track in the one-day game. In fact, Mike Turner and I didn't always agree on our policy in these games. I tended to play people like Paul Haywood, who helped us to save 10 and 15 runs in the field. This, together with our experienced bowlers who could bowl length and line, contained the opposition to reasonable scores which we could cope with; meanwhile our batsmen were growing in confidence, and getting used to playing longer innings – getting used to playing winning cricket, in short.

Mick Norman joined us from Northamptonshire. He was an outstanding cover point, and while as a batsman he was what we call a 'nudge' player, his batting was a luxury we could afford because we never had to get too many runs. We consciously set out to do well in the one-day game because it was as good a way as any to get a team used to winning. When I first went to Grace Road, like most experienced players, I suppose I was rather against the one-day stuff. But I said to the side: 'If we've got to play it, we might as well play it properly and get some of the rewards for winning. You will get a bit of money out of it and it will do everybody a bit of good in every way.' There was another reason for our concentration on success in the one-day game: in 1969 the pitches at Grace Road were very slow, 'nothing' wickets, and it was going to be damn near impossible to win a three-day game there. In the one-day game the pitch was obviously going to have substantially less effect on the course of the game; we had as much chance of winning as anyone else and that was what the team had to get into their heads – that we were capable of beating anybody, provided we played it right.

We might even have done well in the championship, despite the Grace Road wicket, because after a month together training before the start of the season we had a great team spirit going and we were, in fact, second in the championship when I was chosen as captain of England. So while this was good for the prestige of Leicestershire it took away the experience and the leadership for which they had signed me. Frankly, by the time I had played three Tests and the one-day internationals and returned to my county, I couldn't believe it was the same side I had left behind. Unfortunately, Maurice Hallam was not accepted by some of the senior players and I found the team spirit had melted away. We managed to get it together again by the end of the season, but because I was away so much it was a near-impossibility for us to be a winning side. This continued so long as I was playing for England, and again it was going to be much easier to do well in the one-day competitions because I could take part in more of these games. Our first success was delayed until 1972, when we beat Yorkshire in the Benson and Hedges Cup final. We finished second in the John Player League, too, but it was the B & H which, to me, was the turning point.

I was probably more nervous about that final than about any cricket match I had ever played in. We had worked very hard for three years to get something going at Leicester, despite my absences on Test duty and one or two other minor problems; so I suppose I was nervous that, if we had come this far and then we failed at this hurdle, it might take us another two years or more to get back to people believing in themselves. This was to be the vital breakthrough.

It was one of those low-scoring games which we had learned to play. Boycott was out of the Yorkshire side with a smashed thumb, and Philip Sharpe was captain. He was perhaps a bit unlucky to win the toss because it was one of those wickets with just a touch of green in it. He thought about it a long time and then batted. If I had been him I would have put us in, especially when he had Tony Nicholson, Chris Old, Howard Cooper and Richard Hutton to use the seam and John Woodford to back them up. But it was a very difficult decision for Philip. They batted, as it was, and only scored 136. Even so, we had five down for 97 and then the sun came out and conditions eased just a bit so that we knocked them off without losing another wicket.

Chris Balderstone got 41 not out, and that must have been a bit of a blow to Yorkshire, though perhaps not to those who let him go and who never seem to learn. I'll come back to 'Baldy' in a minute, but already at Leicester when I went there, was one Yorkshireman who must have thought long and hard. Jack Birkenshaw had left Yorkshire after the 1960 season because he felt it was going to be difficult to get a chance to develop with me established in the side. Consequently, I am sure he felt very disappointed when he heard that I was to follow him to Leicester. I would certainly have been a bit down if I had been in his shoes. So I took the first opportunity to tell him: 'I'm thirty-six, going on thirty-seven. I want you to do more bowling than me if need be so don't worry. You'll get a fair crack of the whip.' And in fact in that first season, 1969, he bowled more than twice as many overs as me and he scored nearly a thousand runs as well. He has always been a useful batsman and he eventually fought his way into the one-day side by becoming a fine timer of the ball. He missed out a bit in the early stages because he has never been the fastest thing on two legs, but that's not Jack's fault. He has always trained hard and kept himself fit; he is simply not a naturally quick mover.

Chris Balderstone joined us from Yorkshire because he was very much the type of player I wanted in the side. He had been with Yorkshire for eight or nine years without ever getting a regular place, but I knew he was a sound batsman and we hadn't a regular slow left-armer in the side at Leicester. But most of all it was Chris's attitude that I wanted. He was a complete professional in his approach to sport. He had been a league soccer player for years and he had that hardness which is part of the will-to-win. At the same time, Chris kept this hidden beneath the exterior of the thoroughly nice bloke that he has always been. But I knew the hardness was there; Chris could be as tough as anyone.

Ken Higgs's arrival was rather different. He had retired from Lancashire after 1969 and when Mike Turner and I were discussing our need for another experienced fast bowler we went through just about every name we could think of. We combed through *Wisden*, looked through every reference book and list of names we could think of, and finally it was Mike who said, 'I wonder if we could tempt Higgs back from the League?' He had a chat with Ken, and talked him into returning to first-class cricket and I was delighted. He was just the type we needed – as strong as a bull, and never turned it in. He was a bit temperamental at times, because he needed to blow up about twice a season and then you had to handle him a bit diplomatically, but he has a big heart, and was always willing to put everything into the game for you.

We had a few disappointments in 1973, dropping down the Championship and John Player tables and going out of the Benson and Hedges Cup in the quarter-final, but my England career finally came to an end that season and I could now really concentrate on my efforts to improve my adopted county. In 1974 we had the nucleus, with McKenzie and Higgs to open the bowling and Terry Spencer proving a very good warhorse, too. He cut a few yards off his run and while he could still be very lively, for the first time in his life he was not trying to knock everybody's head off, and he became a very good bowler for us. Brian Davison was just coming in and he could bowl seam-up. For spin we had Birkenshaw, myself, Balderstone and John Steele coming along, so we had a good all-round attack with most of them able to bat a bit.

We won the John Player and finished fourth in the Championship; we were beginning to feel we could take anybody on, but it was still hard going in the three-day game when we played our home matches at Grace Road. It was still difficult to bowl a side out twice and it was still not too easy to score quickly. However, in 1975 came our vintage year ... we became the first side ever to win the Championship *and* a one-day competition in the same season. It was World Cup year, followed by a tour by the Australians, a summer of almost unbroken golden sunshine. And the sun certainly shone on Leicestershire. Trevor Bailey summed it up like this in the *World of Cricket*:

'First, they were never hampered by international calls. Second, Ray Illingworth led them with truly great skill. Third, their attack was unusually varied and therefore able to exploit all types of conditions. Fourth, although their batting line-up may have been somewhat short of real class, it had both depth and character which showed in the way the tail came to the rescue in time of need, especially in that last vital match against Derbyshire in the middle of September. Finally, they were a team with everyone contributing something in terms of wickets, runs and catches.'

By this time we had got a new groundsman, Lol Spence, at Leicester who did a tremendous job. He got a lot of the rubbish out of the middle and improved the ground out of all recognition;

he kept the wickets good and true, but contrived to get a little bit of pace in them, shaved the ends a bit so that the spinners could come into it, and always the big outfield was in immaculate condition. More centuries were made on the ground in 1975 than on any other in the country. The faster bowlers got enough encouragement to convince them it was worthwhile to put everything into it. And the spinners . . . well, we never got an out-and-out turner, but if you bowled well you could probably pick up four for 50 on the last day or something like that. We had a ground on which we could enjoy playing our cricket and we could play the sort of stuff the public could enjoy watching.

Norman McVicker played a major part in our Benson and Hedges final win, taking the first four Middlesex wickets. Apart from Mike Smith, who scored more than half their total of 146, no one ever got in. A remarkable character, Norm McVicker. He played for Lincolnshire and Warwickshire, then joined us when he was well into his thirties. He was far from being the world's worst bowler of medium-fast seamers; he could put his head down and graft with the bat when it was required and he could hit sixes when they were needed – for example, two off the last two balls of a John Player League match to beat Somerset. My old friend D. B. Close nearly died of apoplexy on that occasion! I suppose it was as a dressing-room character as much as anything that Norman will be remembered. He was rarely without a cheerful smile and he was always a tremendous booster of morale, and we were all delighted to see him get the Gold Award in that final of 1975.

After that, we had nearly six weeks run-in to the last games of the County Championship but by then we had no doubts about our own ability. I think we could have beaten anybody in August and September of 1975. Sadly, though, Graeme McKenzie was by now ever so slightly over the hill and we had to leave him out of some of those end-of-the-season matches and everyone felt it. But when we called him into the committee room to tell him what had been decided – there was no question of leaving out a player of 'Garth's' stature without explaining matters – he said, like the great gentleman he was throughout his career: 'It's the right decision. I haven't enjoyed being crashed through the covers after ten to fifteen years at the top, and I realise that I have to be left out.' All the same, we were delighted to have him back with us for the final game of the season – against Derbyshire at Chesterfield – at which the title was won.

Chris Balderstone will remember the game, too; apart from scoring a century and playing a major part in bowling out Derbyshire in their second innings, he took off his pads on the Monday night (he was not out), and drove to Doncaster with Stan Anderson, Rovers' manager, to play in a Football League game!

That was one of the happiest seasons I have ever spent in cricket, not merely because of the results but because of the spirit. Everyone wanted to play. Everyone was willing to give everything, even when he was injured – always provided that the injury was not serious enough to result in his letting the side down. The side was what mattered to everyone and when you get that attitude cricket can be a very happy game.

The Grace Road wicket then got better and better – so much better, in fact, that it became quite impossible to bowl a side out twice. One could make runs, lots of runs, and to win a John Player League game you had to think in terms of a score of around 230. I don't blame Lol Spence for this; he had already worked miracles with the pitch. From being slow and uninteresting, it now had pace, but it was dead true and spinners became less and less effective. Simultaneously we had become such a good side that no one would take a chance by declaring against us, or chasing the targets we set. (It had become rather like the old days of playing for Yorkshire!) So it was particularly annoying to see the pitches at Lord's, say, where a workmanlike team could finish a game in two days. If one day was lost to the weather, it was still possible to squeeze a win out of it.

I firmly believe that if our wickets at home had been something less than perfect we could have won more championships, because we were a very good team indeed and despite our disadvantages, there wasn't much in it at the end of the following seasons. We were only twenty-five points behind in 1976, for instance, and together with Northants we lost fewer matches than anyone else. We won a John Player League and lost two on arithmetical knockouts. I hope it is not unreasonable of me to have left Leicestershire with a feeling of tremendous pride. Nine years earlier we had been a chopping-block for everyone and anyone; by the end of 1978 we were respected by every other county in England.

Those slide-rule finishes prompt the thought that there must be a better way of deciding the John Player League. It seems to me completely unsatisfactory that when you have slogged your guts out all season you finish level with another county and then have to start counting up wins, then away wins, and finally, if necessary (and it has been necessary), working out run-rates. There must be a better way and I am all for having a play-off. It would certainly bring in a lot of money. Suppose, for instance, Leicestershire were involved in a tie at the top with one of the West Country sides. The logical place for a play-off would be Edgbaston. They could get there up the motorway in an hour; Leicestershire would be able to reach Birmingham in forty minutes. Such a match would certainly attract a twenty thousand crowd. Similar neutral grounds could be worked out for whoever was involved, and I am certain it would bring a full house. This is money which is there for the taking, and cricket cannot afford to lose opportunities like that. If three counties were involved we could have a three-way play-off staged on Friday, Saturday and Sunday and I am sure that would pick up £70,000. This is money which cricket needs; we are crying out for more cash.

One of the most satisfying aspects of my years at Leicester was the opportunity to watch, and play a part in, the development of so many young players. We always went for a blend of the experienced men who were 'imported' and cricketers of talent and promise who were developed. Roger Tolchard's greatest progress was made as a batsman. I think he will be the first to admit that he has never been much more than an average wicket-keeper, but he has always been a great competitor, especially with the bat. In particular he has become a very good one-day player and I have, in fact, always enjoyed batting with him. He's a fine runner and I reckon I am a pretty good judge of a run, so when we were together the game was always moving. It was only when we found ourselves running a lot of threes that old age began to manifest itself but on the short singles – and there are always a lot of those involved when Tolly is batting – I didn't find any problems.

Mind you, I have to add that I did not agree with Tolchard's selection as a second wicket-keeper for the 1978–79 tour to Australia. I would have gone for someone like David Bairstow (who was actually flown out to join the party when Tolly was injured) because while he, too, is a useful performer with the bat and has improved tremendously over the last few years, he is a better 'keeper. I would always go for the better man in the specialist position.

David Gower's development was one of the most exciting transitions I have ever seen. Although he was born in Tunbridge Wells and was educated in Canterbury, his was not the case of Kent missing out on a young player of the highest promise. He really came to Leicestershire through the sheer accident of his parents living in Loughborough at the time David was emerging as 'the most exciting English-born batsman to appear ... in the last decade', as *World of Cricket* put it.

He really came right out of the blue as far as I was concerned. I hadn't, of course, seen him play schools cricket, and I had had no opportunity to watch him in the Leicestershire second team; but I was very much aware of the reports coming back from second eleven matches about this dazzling left-hand strokemaker. My first glimpse of him came when the players assembled for the start of the 1975 season. Gower was barely eighteen and right away I knew that here was something very special and yet, ironically, I still have an abiding memory of him in those first few days as just about the worst player of spin-bowling I have ever seen! In the nets, where the ball turned a bit, you would get him out three balls out of four – but at the same time he had great flair as a striker of the ball, and he was a wonderful timer of his strokes. He was lucky to play on good wickets at Grace Road to help his development, and we sent him in early in one-day games to give him a chance to play his shots. He has had more than one rollicking for getting out in a silly way, because from the first we impressed upon him that he was a good enough player to get his runs by stroke-making; there was no need for slogging.

His development was such that some of the innings I have seen him play were sheer poetry. Even after twenty-five years in the game I have come out from the dressing-room on to the balcony just to watch him, once he had got to 10 or 15 and was 'in'. His timing is exquisite. After all my years in the game it is difficult not to get a bit blasé at times, but when Gower was going well and I could watch him stroke the ball away with such perfect timing that it would crash back from the fence around a ninety-yard boundary – well, quite simply, it was thrilling to watch him. For all his abundant natural ability, David has worked tremendously hard at his game and in my final season with Leicestershire I bowled with Jack Birkenshaw at him on a turning pitch in the Lord's nets and never once got him out – that's how much he had improved, and he had accomplished it by working on his own game. The development of David Gower was one of the most exciting experiences in my whole playing career.

He was a good and quick learner and fortunately for him we could always arrange nets at Leicester where the pitch was a slow turner. I think I could play spinners well on that sort of pitch and so could Birkenshaw – we had been brought up on them – and David learned a lot by watching. We gave him a certain amount of advice about where he was playing wrongly and how he might play better and we certainly gave him a lot of stick about concentrating more. Birkie, I'm sure, helped him a lot. I can remember David playing a rather casual shot in a championship match and Jack getting up and shouting at him from the balcony, 'Gower . . . !' It was a sort of growled shout which was nevertheless audible all over the field with the implication of its tone quite unmistakable. David looked up in the middle. He understood.

I hammered him, too, about concentration. I have known him get out stupidly and gone to him in the dressing-room simply to ask, 'Do I have to say anything?' He has replied, 'No', so then all I had to add was, 'All right, then', and walk away. He was that sort of lad. Because we got him when he was very young and 'hammered' him for a year I think it has made him capable of playing big innings. The raw material was always there, right from our first glimpse of him, and I think we moulded it pretty well at Leicestershire. Gower can have a very big Test future.

Les Taylor, the fast bowler who came to us from the coalfields, is a comparatively late developer so he hasn't got time to stand still. Yet with a bit of improvement in two respects he has enough natural ability to go to the top. He is naturally very strong in the shoulders but not in the legs, and in his first couple of seasons he tended to tire after 15 or so overs. I think he needs to do a bit of running and to carry out other leg-strengthening exercises. Also, he came to us just a little bit chest-on. We got him round to some extent but he still needs to get even more side-on when he's delivering. Les was nearing his mid-twenties when he came into the first-class game, so he hasn't much time to play with in bringing about these improvements, but he is a prospect of considerable ability.

Jonathan Agnew is one of the quickest bowlers I have seen come into the game since Fred Trueman burst on to the scene and that was in 1949! He is not like Fred in build – more like Bob Willis. He is tall, and as a teenager, he was still a bit gangling when I first saw him: but he was quick. He came to us from Uppingham School, where Les Berry (the former Leicester batsman) was coach and when we were looking round for someone Les said, 'Yes, he's quick, but he's still young and growing, so don't kill him'. We needed a fast bowler badly because Ken Higgs had some cartilage trouble, and Les Taylor had gone in the thigh. We were in with a chance of the 1978 John Player League and we were strapping both of them up to play on Sundays and resting them during the week. Mike Turner, the Leicester secretary, said, 'We can't play Agnew because it's necessary to notify all the other counties and to tell Lord's and there isn't time'. 'Well', I said, 'seventeen 'phone calls shouldn't take more than half-an-hour. Let's make the effort.' So Mike started 'phoning round and the all-clear came through from Lord's on the Saturday morning we were due to meet Lancashire: Agnew played.

He was raw, of course, but he was excitingly fast. We made Lancashire follow on, so although he only bowled 12 overs in the day, Agnew was jiggered when he came off and I told him, 'Now, what you've got to do is get yourself fit for first-class cricket and if you can the sky's the limit'. And that's so. There isn't another genuinely quick bowler on the horizon.

Another fine player at Grace Road who could go right to the top is Nigel Briers. He is another player whose arrival for full-time duty was a bit delayed because he took a university degree, but I think he has a lot of ability – enough to go *right* to the top.

15

GROUNDS FOR SATISFACTION-AND COMPLAINT

Every cricketer has a favourite ground – I think mine would be Dover, obviously for personal reasons. The sun has always seemed to shine there, for me as well for cricket itself, and I can remember enjoying my game there almost more than anywhere else. But the general deterioration in grounds and their wickets over the past twenty or twenty-five years has had a significant effect on the quality of the game. In the main, wickets are not as good as they used to be, or perhaps I should say not as natural as they used to be. There has been an increasing use of heavy, artificial loams which provide an easy way out for groundsmen. They don't produce bad pitches, so there is not much danger of being reported to Lord's, and groundsmen generally have tended to settle for that. But at the same time these loams do not produce positively good wickets on which an attractive (and exciting – the two usually go together) game can be expected.

Going through the counties in 1978 and 1979 you get only two or three counties where there are, in my view, good wickets, and some of them are even too good at the death. By that I mean they *stay* too good and are utterly predictable right to the end so that the spectator is robbed of the unexpected, of a sudden change in the fortunes of one team, or at any rate a change in the way the game is going.

Predictable cricket is very rarely exciting cricket. It is in the unexpected changes in the way a game flows that one of the basic attractions of cricket is provided. Let's take, first of all, Worcester, which for many years has been one of the best batting wickets in the country. If they make a good wicket with a bit of pace at Worcester you know that the game is very probably going to be drawn over three days. I personally don't think that is a good cricket wicket. My own view is that good wickets should be prepared so that there is pace on the first two days and a bit of bounce, thus enabling batsmen to play their shots because the ball is coming on to the bat, but at the same time testing their technique because of that pace and because of the bounce. If those same wickets are shaved a little bit at the ends, the spinners are able to come into it on the third day instead of being condemned to a role in which they bowl defensively, close up one end if they can and get rid of the overs so that their county is not involved in penalty clauses at the end of the season. Spin bowlers should be attacking bowlers who can bowl defensively if necessary. They absolutely should not be people brought in specially to use up overs by bowling defensively.

Spin bowling is an art in its own right, and should be used as such, as often as possible as a positive means of attack. It is one of the most basic attractions of cricket to see a class spinner in action in conditions which are not impossible for the batsman yet which are, to some extent, helpful to the bowler. That's all he needs ... conditions which are 'helpful' plus three or four expert catchers in close fielding positions around the wicket. And that is the sort of picture I have always felt made the third day of a first-class match one of deep fascination. Two great fast bowlers operating in tandem is, too true, one of the great sights of cricket and at Test match level it is still good to see. But these days, sad to say, most counties are pushed to find one genuinely fast bowler, let alone two, and yet most of them have a pair of spinners – ideally a slow left-armer and an off-spinner to work together. This is the combination to restore to cricket its position as a game of charm, of variety, of extra dimensions. Heaven alone knows the spinner suffers from defensive attitudes created by a negative approach to one-day cricket, of which we have so much today; when he is hamstrung in the three-day game too, by eternally easy-paced wickets which never take spin, cricket is well on the way to destroying its own charm.

We were lucky at Leicester in 1975 when, in a very hot summer, we got good cricket wickets – fast on the first day, slowing just a bit on the second and giving a bit of help to the spinners on the final day. We had a marvellous season of good cricket (quite apart from winning the championship), in which every game went to the last day with exciting finishes as a result. But quite honestly, I could not name more than three or four grounds where you might achieve that – Worcester is one, perhaps, Leicester is another, Middlesborough (the wicket has been good in the last two or three years), Hove (Sussex could probably enjoy such games) – but after that I am struggling to think of another. Scarborough is probably one I should think about because I used to do quite well there myself in the fourth innings. Scarborough is a good *natural* wicket because it has not, over the years, had a lot of rubbish dumped on it to kill it as a cricket pitch. Because Scarborough is beside the sea it always used to 'do a bit' anyway; it usually had a bit of grass on it to start, and then would help me on the last day. But in the state of a pitch on the last day of a county championship match, you have the answer to all the questions which are asked about the future of first-class cricket.

On a pitch which starts easy-paced and becomes more so as the game progresses, captains are not going to make what are known as 'sporting declarations'. Mostly these amount to nothing more than suicide on pitches where the fielding side has to rely on a mistake by the batsman to have any hope of breaking through. If the wicket is starting to turn then a captain can make a declaration which gives both sides a chance of winning. It then becomes a matter of the batsman's technique and/or experience against the bowler's guile (and the fielding captain's know-how) and the result is utterly fascinating cricket. Cricketers don't play out draws on the final day because they want to; in truth, they are even more bored by that sort of outcome than the public, which might come as something of a surprise! Cricketers want to be involved in a contest; they want to pit their skills against those of the opposition for all three days of a match. They don't want to be involved in third-day stagnation any more than the public want to watch it.

However, the county championship is still the competition most cricketers believe cricket is all about, and they have a duty therefore to all the other sixteen counties involved not to lose if they cannot win themselves. That has to be understood. By giving away a game with a quixotic declaration, a county with nothing at stake itself can give another one a walk-in to the title – and we all have too much respect for each other ever to want to do that. So it is really up to county committees (with expert guidance from players, because that is always available) to ask groundsmen to prepare good *cricket* wickets. The players will do their stuff. They still want to win the county championship more than any of the one-day competitions, because they feel it is the ultimate test of skill. In passing, one might add that it is still, in these days of heavy sponsorship, the most profitable contest to win and that, of course, counts for a good deal. But to sustain a winning sequence over a period of something like four months requires ability, and in some cases reserve strength in depth; it needs application, concentration, imagination, and staying-power. It is the one contest we all want to win.

In the last analysis it is cricket's authorities which have to agree that we need the right sort of pitches to play on. Even at Test level things are far from perfect, with Lord's leading the way. In two years I played five or six times at Lord's (Tests and other matches) and I didn't play on one good wicket. Finally I wrote a captain's report which said, 'If Bert Lock had spent more time at Lord's than Leicester we might have got better wickets at Headquarters'. I wrote that report with a certain amount of acidity, in the hope of getting something done – because as a county captain one seems to spend an inordinate amount of time filling in forms of which no one takes the slightest notice. What happened? Freddie Brown wanted to 'do' me for bringing the game into disrepute! How he felt I was doing that, or how he felt he could institute action against me, on remarks made in a confidential report, I don't know; but more and more one feels oneself to be up against attitudes which simply do not begin to be on the same wavelength.

I found a rather marvellous book recently, published in 1926, called *A Searchlight on English Cricket*, and written with coy anonymity by A County Cricketer. One chapter in it deals with the arrival of the fourth Lord Harris (Oxford University and Kent) to take over the Governorship of Bombay. He promptly organised a cricket team, the Bombay Government House XI, and it was, says our author: '...led by Lord Harris himself, much to the disgust of the usual crowd of nobodies who wrote to the Press to say they understood Lord Harris had been sent to India to govern and not to play cricket – as though, forsooth, it is possible to govern anywhere or anybody without first teaching them a bit of cricket!'

There is even better stuff to come: 'But his Lordship only jutted his chin out further', continues Chapter 6 of this delightful publication, 'metaphorically told the grousers to go and stalk Bombay Duck, and continued to prove that unless people play cricket as often as possible they cannot expect to be happy, or to lead clean lives'. I think that is absolutely superb, and I can't help wondering if Freddie Brown wrote it.

Again, at The Oval we had played for years with a large tree growing at the Vauxhall end and causing increasing problems because there was no sightscreen. Captains' reports were filed year after year pointing out these problems but, as ever, nothing was done. It seems simply impossible to get through to the authorities, and yet the forms still have to be filled in. Eventually I wrote that this might have been good enough for Sir Jack Hobbs but it wasn't good enough for me!

Subsequently, my comments had the effect of the seats (in what John Arlott calls the 'Chad stand') being painted duck-egg blue. This was an improvement, but would it have happened if I had continued, and other county captains had continued, to couch their reports in neutral, inoffensive terms? I am sure it wouldn't. I suppose the ultimate irony was when I discovered later that in Jack Hobbs's day there *was* a sightscreen at the Vauxhall end!

But what is the point of filling in these forms if no one takes any notice? What is the point of thrashing out answers to such problems after debating them at length at captains' meetings, if no action follows? If no one is going to take any action, if no one is even going to take any *notice*, we might as well tear up every form we get and drop it in the nearest waste-paper basket.

However, let me end this section on grounds and pitches on a happier note, by returning to places I at least have always liked. It's always a pleasure to play on nice grounds in picturesque settings. Dover came into this category because I always felt the setting was delightful and, as I have said, the sun always seemed to shine. Worcester, too, has a glorious backcloth of the cathedral, and the willows along the River Severn, and it has been a happy hunting-ground for me. My career-best performance occurred there in 1957 – I took nine for 42 for Yorkshire against Worcestershire, with J. H. Wardle bowling at the other end! You are never going to forget a ground where that happens!

What I have never been able to enjoy is playing anywhere in cold, drizzly conditions. I am sure the Almighty never intended that cricket should be played in anything but golden sunshine, especially if the wicket was doing a bit. Yet the sun has rarely shone on cricket at Bradford, where I have enjoyed some of the most fascinating cricket of my life on a wicket which was so natural it almost reached into the realms of the *super*natural at times. Against Hampshire at the end of June, 1962, we were as good as beaten when they reached 156 for five in the fourth innings, wanting 163 to win. Brian Sellers, the king of Yorkshire cricket, had gone home in disgust at five o'clock, so he missed Yorkshire's victory by five runs at a quarter past five. The last five wickets fell for one run and a match which was hopelessly lost was suddenly and dramatically won. Can any other game provide a finish like that?

16

UMPIRES-THE BEST IN THE WORLD?

Captains have a great responsibility to the game, and to the umpires themselves, to give the most serious and conscientious thought to their 'marking' of the way umpires carry out their duties. During my playing career there was a system of awarding marks out of ten; these reports then went to Lord's and if an umpire was consistently getting low marks his suitability was reviewed. Conversely, of course, the men with the best marks over sustained periods joined the Test panel and stood in other games of major importance – Gillette and Benson and Hedges finals, and World Cup games – known in the trade as 'special' matches.

At one time it seemed to me that there was a certain amount of variation in the marking and this appeared to work, roughly, on a regional basis. Consequently, an umpire who got a lot of matches in the south often seemed to get quite different markings from one who had a preponderance of games in the north. I am not saying one area's captains were more critical than another's, or one more easygoing, but there were variations which seemed to be regional in their origin. So I brought this up at a captains' meeting, suggesting that we start with a mark of six as a central, or average, point and worked up or down from there. Perhaps there were still a few variations after that but at least we had more consistency because now all captains were working from the same basic point. There would still be one or two people with an 'anything-for-a-quiet-life' attitude who would always award six so that they did not have to provide explanations or justifications. Now that merely meant that no great harm was done, and the *status quo* was maintained. The real point was that we had, at last, a desirable degree of consistency.

It has always seemed important to me that marking should be

done with care and with thought. I know that if ever we had been involved in a controversial match, I would take the form away with me and not complete it until the following day when, perhaps, I had calmed down a bit. It is only fair to the umpire, and to everyone else concerned, that you give a sane and balanced opinion, not one reached in the heat of the moment. I used to award one mark for the way an umpire was turned out and the way he conducted himself and the game on the field. I always felt that was worth one mark in itself and some people came into the category and some didn't. I never particularly marked an umpire down unless a lot of decisions went wrong. For instance, I did not have any complaint if he missed the odd one which resulted from a faint tickle going somewhere close to the batsman's arms or from an inside edge – the sort of thing that a bowler often doesn't know about himself. That, as far as I was concerned, came within the area of simple human fallibility. What I did mark an umpire down for was getting the wrong line on lbw decisions. I believe that a man who is standing still with a perfect view of the straight line between wicket and wicket should not make mistakes about decisions like that. Umpires know that if there is any doubt at all they should say 'not out' and that gives them a bit more latitude.

Having said that, let me add that I think it is just as bad for an umpire to stand all day saying 'not out' as it is to give a batsman out when he's not. You are asking diligent attention from an umpire at all times, conscientious thought and judgement in his decision-making, and very few errors on line. There should not be very much room for doubt about the line.

It is customary to regard English umpires as the best in the world, and I think that as we have a bigger panel of top-class men than any other country this is natural enough. I am not saying that there have not been, in my time, umpires in overseas countries who could rate with our best; on the other hand, in Australia during the 1970–71 tour you would have been pushed to find a couple who were capable of officiating competently in a Test match at all and generally this is true overseas.

I do not believe it is possible for an English umpire to get right to the top in our game unless he *is* very good. From time to time, in umpiring circles, one hears rumbling about 'favouritism'.

Certainly some umpires believe that some of the others are favoured for one reason or another and Cec Pepper, who never got on to the Test panel, left the first-class umpire's life in 1979 with a whole series of broadsides directed at quite a few of his colleagues. But my own view is that no one would get on to the panel if he were not really very good. What has happened occasionally is that an umpire has reached the top, become rather cocky and decided that he 'knew it all' and been returned whence he came. Most of those who suffered that fate got a bit more sense and subsequently returned to the panel because in basic terms they *were* good umpires.

Pepper, despite his great ability as a player (he must have been one of the best cricketers never to play in a Test for Australia), and the extrovert personality which made him a bit of a character, would not have been one of my own choices for the top. Frankly, I think he lacked the necessary concentration. Here I think one ought to stress just how much hard work is necessary to focus the attention totally and completely on each individual delivery through six long hours of a hot summer's day: the sheer physical demands are quite tremendous in themselves, because standing absolutely still is a good deal more difficult (and often harder on the feet) than running about with, or after, the ball. It really is very, very hard work indeed.

When you add to that the need to rivet the attention, six times an over, to the point where the bowler's feet are at the point of delivery, where his feet land on his follow-through, where the ball pitches and where it progresses after pitching, whether it grazes the edge of the bat (or did it flick the batsman's flannels or pad-strap?) and whether the wicket-keeper or fieldsman catches it cleanly – just try to imagine yourself doing all that for six hours a day, and you begin to get some idea of what it is like to be a first-class umpire.

Pepper liked to be involved with the players and the game more than most umpires; he also liked to be involved in 'chat' during a game, and if his conversational sallies happened to coincide with moments of decision-making there were batsmen, and bowlers, who did not always appreciate the gregarious nature of the big Aussie.

His fellow countryman, Bill Alley, comes into the category, I think, of one of those who got to the top and fell from grace. He is one of the best liked men in the game, who was tremendously respected as a player during an exceptional career and I was probably one of the strongest 'pushers' for him to go on to the Test panel. I always liked Bill as a man and I respected him as an umpire at the time I was commending him, partly because he was not afraid to give an lbw decision when the batsman was on the front foot. But having reached the top, I think he became a little more of a chatty Australian and a little less of a sternly-concentrating Test umpire.

Other umpires had other problems. In 1978 in a game at Taunton, Brian Rose asked for a guard of 'middle' and after a rather adventurous over he asked one of the visiting side to check the guard. It was outside the leg stump! This is the sort of story which goes round the circuit so everyone began to watch the social habits of that particular official who was reported at another ground to have drunk eight double whiskies during the lunch and tea intervals. In another match the same chap was in such a state that at the end of a day's play he could not remember where he had left his car and had to be driven round and round the town by his colleague, looking for it. He was still on the list in 1979.

During my career the best umpire of all was Syd Buller – there is no doubt in my mind about that at all. Apart from being technically excellent, he had great authority on the field in a completely unobtrusive manner. There was nothing hectoring or abrasive about him, but no one was ever in the slightest doubt about who was making the decisions. That was a characteristic of outstanding importance, because captains who seek to influence umpires in a variety of ways are not unknown. There are captains who spend a great deal of time during a game nipping in and out of the umpires' room, ostensibly to ask an innocuous question, but they can still find time to toss in an oblique remark about some aspect of the game.

There are some umpires who go on for years, never being dropped from the list yet never getting what they call a 'special' match – a Test, a Cup final, a World Cup game – and this is a little puzzling to some students of the game. Ron Aspinall, for instance, the former Yorkshire fast bowler, has been on the first-class list since 1960 without standing in anything but run-of-the-mill games. I think perhaps Ron is a better umpire now than he was in the earlier days of his career when I considered him to be 'not very good'. In a game at Canterbury I was bowling round the wicket but getting a lot of turn and Jimmy Binks and I kept shouting for lbw but every appeal was turned down. That evening over a pint, Jimmy and Jackie Hampshire asked Ron what had been wrong with the appeals and he said: 'Well, Illy's bowling round the wicket, his arm's a bit low, I don't think he can straighten it enough to get an lb.' And Binkie and I were convinced that some had turned enough to beat the *leg* stump! So Ron had stood at my end with a completely preconceived idea about lbw appeals, apparently without concentrating on each individual delivery and its line. That is what made Ron, to me, not one of the best umpires even if he wasn't, outright, a bad one. After nineteen consecutive years on the list, I imagine that what has happened is that captains have considered his performance, thought 'Well, he's a nice fellow but ...' and marked him just below average – not so far below as to cause him to be dropped, but never high enough to get him into the top bracket.

Getting to the top is just as important to umpires today as it is to players, because apart from the prestige (which can lead to all kinds of fringe benefits) the financial rewards are considerable, thanks to the Cornhill Insurance sponsorship of Test match cricket – £750 per match in 1978, £900 in 1979. As with the players' money, I am not quite sure there is a fair and equitable distribution of this new income. I think perhaps just a little bit too much has gone to the top and not quite enough to the lower orders of the game. The umpire's seasonal wages have gone up to something like £4,000 a summer, and I have been glad to see this. It was right that enough money should be made available to draw the right sort of men into the job, and we have seen the benefit with men in their early forties coming on to the list. This is what we have needed because it is a job which needs a good deal of physical fitness as well as mental alertness.

As I have said, I believe our general standards are the best in the world although that view has not always been shared by overseas players. The name of Frank Chester is revered in English cricket as the greatest of all umpires, but don't tell the Australians that. They can reach new heights of invective at some of their memories of the great man and there have also been periods when bowlers might have been forgiven for thinking that certain specialist batsmen/captains were granted personal immunity from the penalties of the lbw law. Sonny Ramadhin wakes up at night screaming at the memory of Edgbaston, 1957, when he claims Peter May and Colin Cowdrey simply kicked their way to a stand of 411 for the fourth English wicket in the second innings. And, again in Birmingham, I remember bowling at the two Smiths on a rare turner there. A.C. was in all kinds of trouble and M.J.K. shouted down the pitch, 'Stick your bloody leg down the pitch, A.C.'. Needless to say I hit the pad three or four times an over after that but never got any response to my shout.

Three or four of our umpires are outstanding. These are 'Dickie' Bird, Barry Meyer and David Constant – although Constant was one of those who became a bit over-confident after getting to the top. But now he has settled down to being a really first-rate umpire again. Then you get men like Lloyd Budd, who does a pleasant job all the time, doesn't make many mistakes, probably won't stick his neck out by 'giving' too much, but basically does a sound job. Yes, I think in general we are more than fortunate in the standard of umpiring in this country: long may it continue.

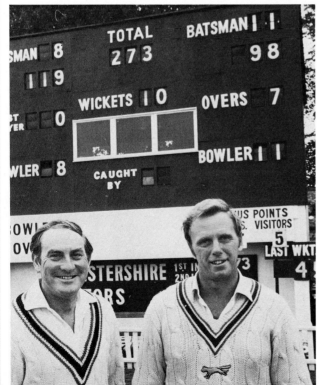

Above: Ouch! But it sticks, and Doug Walters is out, bowled Snow, 1. Lord's, 1972. (Sport & General)

Left: Quite a useful last-wicket partnership with Ken Higgs at Grace Road . . . (Leicester Mercury)

Left: A very rare picture of F. S. Trueman in the role of listener. (Leicester Mercury)

Below left: Leicestershire - County Champions, 1975.
Back row, l to r: Roger Tolchard, Barry Dudleston, David Gower, Chris Balderstone, Brian Davison, John Steele.
Front row, l to r: Jack Birkenshaw, Ken Higgs, Ray Illingworth, Graeme McKenzie, Norman McVicker.

Right: Benson and Hedges Cup winners; Lord's, 1975. (Patrick Eagar)

Below: A happy family group Diane, Vicky and Shirley relax with me at home.

Overleaf: John Player League winners, 1977. Celebrations at Grace Road. (Leicester Mercury)

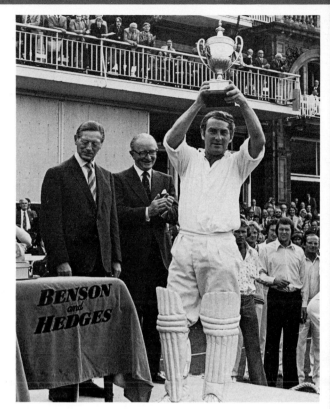

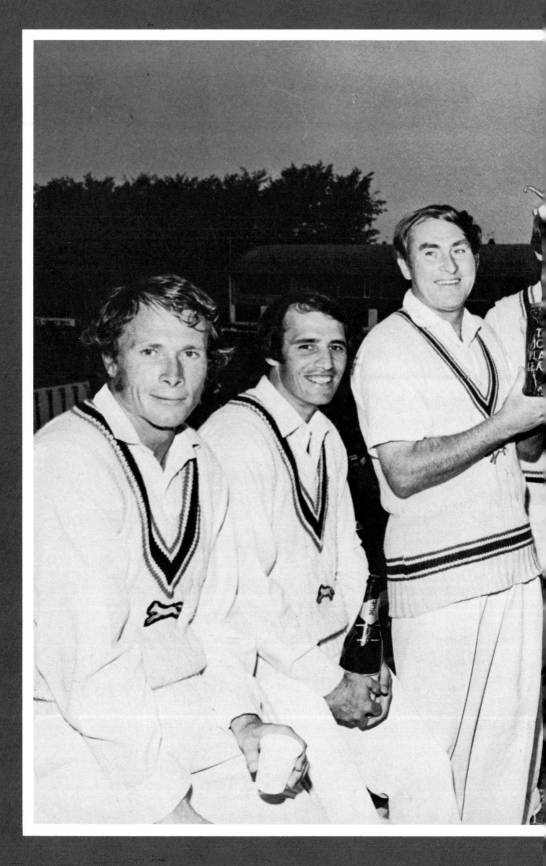

Above left: Raymond
Illingworth, CBE. With Shirley and
the girls at Lord's, accompanied
by the then England women's
captain, Rachael Heyhoe-Flint.
(Daily Express)

Left: A civic reception and inscribed
salver from the mayor of Pudsey.

Above: The classic off-spinner in
attack - right arm round the
wicket. (Patrick Eagar)

Above: HRH The Prince of
Wales (wearing a Lord's
Taverners' tie) in quizzical mood.
(Leicester Mercury)

17

THE RECONCILIATION

The opportunity to return to Yorkshire came more or less out of the blue, and when it did come I had to do an awful lot of heart-searching. Once a Yorkshireman, always a Yorkshireman and I had never been any less a Yorkie for my move to the Midlands. I thought my cricket in the way that my childhood and my formative years had taught me. My whole outlook and my approach to the game were characteristically Yorkshire, and if I need to explain exactly what that is, perhaps I can best illustrate it with a little tale involving Freddie Trueman. As he walked out on to a Test field in Australia at the resumption of a match which was slipping away from England, Fred muttered to no one in particular – thinking aloud, really, 'Come on, now. Let's get stuck into these bastards.' And his captain was moved to comment, 'The trouble with you damn Yorkshiremen is that you are only interested in playing this game to win'. That has remained with Fred as the most astonishing remark he has ever heard uttered on a Test field, and I know how he feels.

So, an invitation to return to manage Yorkshire was obviously a very attractive proposition indeed. At the same time I had become very much involved with Leicestershire. I had seen the ground, for one thing, develop from a 'nothing' sort of place to one of the best playing areas in the country. I had seen the side develop from a chopping-block outfit to one as good as any other in the game. I had seen young players like Gower, Briers and Agnew come on the scene, and the first of those progress to the England side where he was making centuries. It was impossible not to become very involved indeed, in every way, with a county which had made such wonderful progress in ten years. They had been ten wonderful years for me. My wife and daughters, too, liked

Leicester, and personally I had made more close friendships than I had in the time when I was playing for Yorkshire. They are friendships which, I am glad to say, will continue wherever work or play take me in the future.

There had been a certain amount of speculation in newspapers that Yorkshire might be toying with the idea of appointing a full-time cricket manager, but I hadn't taken a great deal of notice. I had even seen my own name mentioned as a possible candidate but at the time I hadn't regarded it as anything more than 'newspaper talk'. Then, out of the blue, came a 'phone call from Michael Crawford, the Yorkshire treasurer, saying he would like to have a word with me. Well, once that had happened, I put two and two together (and, being a Yorkshireman, got five) and began to think there might be something in the offing. I went to Leeds to see Michael, and over a half of beer and a sandwich he asked me if I would be interested in the job. I replied, 'Let me think about it, first, and we'll have another meeting in a few days'.

I came back home and talked everything over, thoroughly, with Shirley, because obviously the family were very much involved in a change like that. Shirley had made good friends in Leicester; and while we had kept our home in Pudsey the question had arisen – and at that stage of my career was going to arise with increasing frequency – of moving our home to Leicester. A great deal was at stake.

Having discussed everything at some length, we decided that the answer would be 'Yes', provided all the relevant details were satisfactory. I rang Michael Crawford and told him my decision. We had a bit of a discussion on the 'phone and I emphasised that the whole matter at this stage had to be confidential. Clearly, until all the details were finalised, I did not want the matter made public.

Now I think this stage of the negotiations needs a certain amount of explanation, because there were rumblings in some quarters about the way they were carried out. My meeting, at which final agreement was reached, was with a small group of the Yorkshire committee – Michael Crawford, the chairman, Arthur Connell, and Norman Shuttleworth. We had discussed terms in a general way on the telephone, as I have said, but at that meeting they came up with figures which were perfectly acceptable to me and it was agreed that I would take the job.

From the start, only about four or five people knew of the negotiations, which brought complaints from within the Yorkshire committee that they had been kept in the dark. Perhaps I was a little bit to blame for that because I insisted, and the county's negotiators were of the same mind, that until we actually reached agreement, it was better to keep the whole business between ourselves.

If our discussions had been reported to the full committee as a formal matter, then thirty or forty people would immediately have become involved. If matters had been dealt with on a formal basis, Leicestershire's committee would have had to know as well, and that would have meant around fifty people knowing something which was vital to my whole future. There is no way then that the matter could have been kept confidential, and, quite frankly, I did not want such a delicate matter being broadcast all round the place. I deplore this sort of thing in football ... reading that so-and-so is 'unsettled', or that one club or another is 'about to move in' with an offer for a player. I think that sort of thing is terrible and I have always thought so.

The original approach had been informal, my first reaction had been off-the-cuff. I wanted to keep it that way until something concrete had been worked out. So – I'm sorry if people were upset. The last thing I ever wanted was to offend anyone in Yorkshire or at Leicester, where I had had ten such very happy years. It was a great wrench to leave behind so much that Mike Turner and I had built up together, but I suppose there comes a time when it is right to move on to something new. As I have said, it was not without a great deal of heart-searching that I finally decided to leave. I was very proud of what we had built at Leicester, and I shall always watch events there with very great interest and no little affection.

Ahead of me, now, stretched a new challenge, and one that I could not really resist.

18
THE BOYCOTT AFFAIR

Geoffrey Boycott was not too pleased with the announcement that I was to return to Yorkshire as cricket manager, and it is not difficult to understand how he felt. Nevertheless, his feelings were based on an emotional approach to the matter rather than a logical one, and I made that clear to him from the first. During the 1978 season (when my appointment had been announced to start at the beginning of 1979) he asked me how I would have felt if such an appointment had been made 'over my head' at Leicestershire. My reply didn't take much working out. 'Geoff', I said, 'considering that for the past six or seven seasons Leicestershire have been one of the most successful sides in the country, there was no question of such a situation arising. Now if I had been captain for eight seasons during which the county won nothing and only very rarely looked to be in a position to win anything, I would not have been surprised at all in a new appointment. Why should you be?'

During the course of 1978 I think he came a little towards accepting the appointment in his mind – he had, of course, to accept it as a fact – but in September the committee decided to replace him as captain with John Hampshire and that, understandably, was a body-blow to Geoff.

From the first, Boycott has always been a player who needed to be admired and respected. He was not, like Hampshire, a naturally gifted cricketer. He was a manufactured player. He made himself into the batsman he has become by hard work and concentration and determination. He deserves immense credit for that, because that hard work and concentration and determination created one of the most successful batsmen in the world. It was a tremendous achievement and there are very few people who could have done it. But that success, coaxed from little or no natural stroke-making ability, proved a two-edged sword because Geoff, who has always had an inferiority complex, needed to be told frequently how good he was.

During my earlier days with Yorkshire, when he had already established himself as a regular England opener, he would still aproach Brian Close or Freddie Trueman or myself, seeking reassurance about his ability. I have said to him, more than once: 'Geoff, you are the best player in the country. Get out there and do your stuff.' He needed that boost to his ego whenever things went a little bit wrong, as they go wrong for all of us at times. Once he became captain of Yorkshire, it all began to happen in reverse. As soon as some of the more experienced players had left the side, men like Philip Sharpe, Richard Hutton, Don Wilson and Tony Nicholson, there was no one there who could question the wisdom of some of his actions. But once they had gone, Geoff was left with no one to lean on when the going became tough and soon found that captaincy can be a very lonely job. Thus when he needed someone to tell him that what he had done was right; to tell him how good he was: there was no one left with the stature to do it. What Geoff never seemed to realise, too, was that instead of asking for the admiration of others he needed to be offering that kind of encouragement to his young players. They had their example; they knew how good he was; they had grown up with the greatness of Boycott's scoring achievements; *they* didn't need to be told how good he was, and they certainly didn't expect to have to form an overt admiration society. What they needed was for an established great player to tell them when they had done well, and to be eased along with a bit of advice when they hadn't done so well.

Instead, they read in newspapers and they heard that Geoff had told friends (and sometimes ordinary members of the public) of the burden he had to carry ... that he was the only player in the side with any ability and that he had to 'carry' the other batsmen. In short, Geoff steadily and consistently made a rod for his own back. In some ways it was possible to sympathise with him. To some extent, Yorkshire's success over so many years had been based on a continuity of standards, of policies, of traditions. Young players of promise had been brought into sides packed with senior players of great ability and experience. They had been brought along very gradually and, in their occasional games with the senior side, had slowly picked up the momentum – the style if you like – of life in a county team which was expected as of right to win the County Championship every year, a team against which every other county gave absolutely nothing away and played just a little bit harder. By getting rid of four experienced players who could have stood alongside him and gently introduced the new boys to those traditions, Geoff had made the sternest rod of all for his own back.

The youngsters never learned, as we had learned in the past (and often the hard way) the standards of team discipline and self-discipline which had always been an essential part of York-shire's way of cricket life. Instead, they found only one really senior player, their captain, who seemed to them more interested in making himself into a run-scoring legend than in moulding a team which had to live up to the greatest reputation in cricket. And when they found that this captain, who expected them to look up to him and, indeed, to revere him, was going around saying that they were not very good players at all, then the rot was bound to set in.

So I have got to say that I felt Yorkshire's decision to remove Geoff from the captaincy was the right one. It put me in a slightly difficult position because my new appointment did not officially take effect until 1 April, 1979. Of course, I busied myself during the winter making plans and formulating policy, talking to the committee, to officials and to various sub-committees, but offici-ally I was not in charge until the following spring. Consequently, I was not directly involved in any way with the change of captaincy but I did want to see the matter straightened out before I took over, for obvious reasons.

There was a very nasty three months after the announcement of the change in captaincy which did not reflect much credit on anyone at all, as all kinds of dirty linen was very publicly washed. Newspapers, television and radio were carrying a new instalment in the series virtually every day, and charge and counter-charge were flung across back pages, screens and the airwaves. One producer from the BBC programme *Nationwide* came north knowing a great deal about television but not so much about county cricket and Yorkshire cricket in particular. After three days of filming in the pubs and clubs and streets of the West Riding, he asked in bewilderment: 'Just what is so special about the *Yorkshire* captaincy? Other counties change their captains with a fair degree of regularity but when it happens here it wipes everything else, even soccer, off the sports pages for weeks on end.' One could understand his perplexity, even though to Yorkshiremen in the street the whole row was a natural consequence of the change which had been announced.

Finally, I became involved myself because I was asked to sound out the feeling amongst the senior players. As a result of what I learned I wrote to the committee saying that none of those players was against the change.

This brought an immediate outcry from Geoff's supporters in the Reform Group, and from Geoff himself, that the statement was untrue and that all the players were *not* against his continuing as captain. So let me put this on record: because I was still not officially the cricket manager of Yorkshire, I asked the senior capped player, Geoff Cope, to check with his colleagues. Three players had already gone to Australia (not on the England tour but to play club cricket through our winter) – Bill Athey, Jimmy Love and Kevin Sharp – but as they were not 'capped' players they did not come within the scope of Geoff Cope's check-up. He spoke to all the capped players and gave me the answer: *not one of them is against the change in captaincy.*

Now here again one gets an insight into how Boycott's personality let him down as a captain. One of those senior players who had suffered more than most from Geoff's tongue told me: 'I feel sorry for him at this moment. His whole world has fallen apart in the last twelve months, and it is impossible not to feel a great deal of sympathy for him. But I know damn well that if I change my mind and back him up he will be kicking my teeth in once we get into a new season.' And it's true to say that a lot of people felt exactly that way. Geoff, after achieving a lifetime's ambition by skippering England in one Test against Pakistan and three against New Zealand (when he stepped in for the injured Mike Brearley), had then been deposed from his England vice-captaincy on the 1978–79 tour to Australia, had lost his mother to whom we all knew he was extremely attached, and then, the very next day, had been told that he was being replaced as Yorkshire's captain. All this, in fact, had been crammed into the space of six weeks. Even the most stony-hearted of Geoff's opponents were bound to find it impossible not to feel sorry for him. But that wasn't going to get Yorkshire cricket on its feet again, and we were now approaching the longest period in the county's history without a competitive success. The time had come for a change, and I am bound to say I agreed with that view.

★　　★　　★　　★　　★

John Hampshire was the man chosen to take over from Geoff Boycott, and we all knew that there had been occasions in the past when things had not gone as well under his captaincy as they ought to have done, particularly in his benefit year. On the other hand, I had played against Yorkshire in 1978 when John was captain and the spirit of the team and the atmosphere in the dressing-room were tremendous. In taking over as manager I felt that if we could get something like that going again we would be off to a good start.

Hamps's knowledge of the game and his tactical sense were perhaps not quite as acute as Geoff's. Boycott, as I have said, is very much a manufactured cricketer and consequently has always had to think long and hard about every aspect of the game. John, on the other hand, has always been a much freer maker of strokes and very much less intense in his approach to the game, but in the later seventies I felt he was working on his game much more than he had done in the past. If he had done that earlier, perhaps he might have been a more successful batsman. At the time I was taking over I wasn't a hundred per cent sure that John was as good, technically, in his thinking about the game, but against that he had the confidence to make decisions which Geoff seemed increasingly to lack towards the end of his period as captain. I felt that John would never be afraid to make decisions. Some would be right and some would be wrong, but if you have got a good team spirit and the lads are right behind you, what might perhaps have been a fractionally wrong decision can turn out to be just the right one. So I didn't foresee any difficulties in that direction as I looked forward to my first season as manager.

My precise terms of reference were written into my contract and I did not see any problem in working with the already established officials. Joe Lister, the secretary, said that he did not regard himself as being 'over' me, or me in charge of him. He saw our duties as complementary to each other and there would be occasions when each needed the help of the other. That was the way I saw it too, and that was fine. Doug Padgett, the coach, had been my good friend since we were both kids going to the Yorkshire nets. We had roomed together and driven about the country together for ten years. We knew each other inside out and we could tell each other to get stuffed if the occasion arose without giving or taking personal offence. There was absolutely no possibility of a problem there. But after playing for Yorkshire for seventeen years with a thirteen-man selection committee, I knew only too well the difficulties *that* could create: so from the first it was written into my contract that I would have sole responsibility for picking the first XI, the second XI, and the Under-25 team.

Obviously I was going to work in conjunction with the captain as far as the first team was concerned, and with the coach on the second and under-25s – but the ultimate control was mine. In terms of press releases on team matters, I was again given full responsibility. Here I planned to work in close cooperation with the secretary, because there were going to be times when I was away with the team and he was 'on the spot' at Headingley, to which press inquiries might be addressed. I went over all the areas where our responsibilities touched, with Joe, and we reached agreement without any difficulty.

There was still a big general committee, but we set about streamlining matters here, too. The cricket committee disappeared and we started with a management committee, consisting of the various sub-committee chairmen, plus officials and myself, and six places to which general committeemen would be elected by vote within that committee. That was going to give us a management committee of about fourteen, which I still felt was rather on the big side but at least we were going in the right direction. The idea was that I would report to that management committee about once a month, just as a managing director would report to his board. The new structure came about as a result of a pooling of ideas – a few of mine, a few of the officials' and a few from the general committee. Ideally I would have liked the executive to be down to about eight or nine people, but you can't expect to get everything worked out in minute detail in the space of a few months. I felt we had made progress and in the right direction. There would obviously be problems from time to time which had not been foreseeable; we hoped that they would not be there in the second year of my management.

My first decree, if you like to call it that, was that training for the 1979 season would start a week earlier than usual and that week was to be devoted to physical fitness training at Carnegie College. As a prelude to this, I wrote to all the first team players telling them I expected them to be seventy per cent fit when they arrived. It was going to be a hard week for them in any case; for those who were not even two-thirds fit, it was going to be *bloody* hard. Yorkshire players, frankly, were never very keen on the idea of physical fitness *per se*. I think the belief was always that ability by itself was the all-important factor; from the first, I set out to dispel that illusion, because an illusion is what it was.

Going back to my own days as a Yorkshire player, men like Fred would turn up for the start of the season having done a little bit of token training but nothing serious, and it would take two or three weeks for him to get into the swing of things. All right – in those days there were the traditional 'pipe-opening' games against the MCC and the two universities, and it was possible for those members of the team who were not quite up to scratch to play themselves into form. In 1979 this was far from being the case. It was vital to be right on the top line from the moment the first ball of the season was bowled, because if we lost two or three John Player matches and a couple of Benson and Hedges games we were out of two of the season's four competitions before we had started. So the emphasis for my first season was going to be very much on physical readiness. There was no way I was going to put an unfit, or even semi-fit, Yorkshire on the field in the now vital opening games of a season.

Looking at the forces available, I was reasonably happy about the batting. We had young players of real talent, like Athey, Love and Sharp, to go with the experience of Boycott, Hampshire and

Lumb. One problem, though, was that since Closey and I left, Yorkshire had been short of all-rounders. In addition to the two of us, men like Fred, Don Wilson and Jimmy Binks could usually be relied upon to get runs at one time or another. Since that era the all-round strength of the side had not been the same, although in 1977 and 1978 there had been a certain improvement because Bairstow began to weigh in with quite a lot of runs. But we were still desperately short of batsmen who could take wickets and bowlers who could score runs. At times, many times, Yorkshire had been playing with five batsmen, five bowlers and a wicket-keeper and that didn't provide enough depth in batting.

In one-day cricket there are three distinct phases – batting, bowling and fielding – all of which are of equal importance, and I believe that all players have to be specialists in two of those three departments.

From the first, I was looking very closely at the one-day competitions. Whilst we all love to play championship cricket, particularly the time it gives us to display all the arts and crafts of cricket, one has to face the fact that three out of the four contests involve the one-day game. It was simply being realistic to take a long look at our ability to play well in that sort of game. I firmly believed that this was one area where Yorkshire ought to be the best players in the country. I also believed they should be the best paid in the country. In my earlier days with the county we were certainly the best players, but we were not the best paid at all. So right from the start, as cricket manager, I went through the whole pay structure with the treasurer, and as a result Yorkshire in 1979 started by paying their players absolutely every penny the county could afford – in fact they went just a little further than that and moved beyond the budget which had been produced for wages. As the players went into the new season they knew that given reasonable success they could make not less than £1,000 more than in 1978, and possibly up to £1,500 more.

I have always been a players' man, and I hope I always shall be. Now, treading the tightrope between players and management, I could see there was an obvious danger of paying the players for results before they had been achieved. So the increases were not across-the-board rises; they were incorporated in win-bonuses and incentives so the players were going to have to earn their extra money. In return for these new incentives I told the players I expected something more than results from them. I said I expected them to turn up at grounds smartly dressed; I expected them to look like Yorkshire cricketers and to play like them. Something which Sir Donald Bradman once said when I was a kid has always stuck in my mind. He said, 'If you can't always play like a cricketer you can at least look like one', and that has always seemed to me a very valid point.

The various ramifications of the Boycott affair had already cost the county £12,000, and further legal matters were outstanding which were likely to put the bill up even higher. I am not saying the Reform Group were wrong, or that the various ballots and meetings should never have been held. That's another matter altogether. But the fact remained that the cost of the whole affair put the county in a position where a bit more money for the players was just not available. Nevertheless, they had got a good deal and now it was up to them.

My policy on wages was an extension of my philosophy as England captain – I will back players a hundred per cent, but the maximum effort has got to come from them as well. It has got to be a two-way thing. This has always been an important point to me and I was interested to see Don Revie adopt a rather similar policy when he became manager of Leeds United, a club in which I have always taken a keen interest. It worked successfully for Don and if we can do as well as Leeds United did under his management it will be great.

So I was reasonably satisfied about the strength of the batting as we approached my first season back in Yorkshire. There were other areas where I wanted to see a bit better cover – for instance we were going to have a few problems if David Bairstow was injured. We were a bit thin as far as fast bowling was concerned (who wasn't?) so I had spoken to John Neal, the Middlesbrough football manager, about Alan Ramage and got his promise that Ramage would be available to us, full-time, from 1 May. Ramage had a good action, was quite quick – a bit quicker than Chris Old at times – and we hoped he might make the grade. That was our number one priority – to find a good fast bowler.

In this area I was once again working with Doug Padgett, as I have said, and that was thoroughly good. We decided to make a few changes in our talent-spotting and coaching schemes. People wrote to me from the Huddersfield area, for instance, to say that young players were being overlooked and that it seemed a lad had to play in the Bradford League to have a chance for the county. This was not true, of course, but Doug and I started looking at the possibility of setting up a net in the Huddersfield area so that no one slipped through. Yorkshire is a very big county and we weren't going to get everything right in the first few months, but we had made a start and we were working on new ideas all the time. One thing I hoped I had made clear to everyone – League representatives, schoolmasters, coaches: if they had a youngster who looked promising they had only to write to Headingley and that boy would get a trial. That was a promise. From the education authorities I wanted some feedback in the form of better wickets for schoolboys to play on. By and large, school wickets are deplorable, and young players are never going to learn anything when the ball is flying about all over the place. By speaking at major League dinners I could make my plea to clubs for better facilities for their juniors.

But until we had worked out a way to make an official approach to education committees throughout the county, the initiative was going to have to come from them. If they couldn't provide decent wickets by orthodox preparation, then I hoped to see them lay down artificial pitches as authorities were already doing in other parts of the country. Schools were an essential part of the future of Yorkshire cricket; they had produced the teams of my generation and previous ones. Now with changes in examination dates, new-style curricula, different holiday periods and the whole structure of the school system changing, that production line seemed to have ground to a halt, or very nearly. We had got to get it working again.

I set myself no targets for 1979. With greater emphasis on one-day cricket, the dividing line between victory and defeat had become a very fine one in recent years ... five runs or one wicket or something like that ... and so the element of luck often played a bigger part in getting a result. However, I have always believed that to some extent a team creates its own luck and in this connection, fielding can be of vital importance. There was going to be far greater emphasis on catching and ground fielding in our pre-season sessions, with a view to eliminating a few problems York-shire experienced in this department in recent seasons. With smaller margins between winning and losing a catch or a run-out could make so much difference, and I felt that once we were pushing towards targets of victory, confidence would grow and we might find ourselves in a position to win something.

This was not, I felt, wishful thinking. Most people know that over-optimism is not an Illingworth characteristic. I have always believed that you never get anything without working for it. We had, I felt, most of the talent we wanted; now came the effort required. I went into the 1979 season telling myself no more than this: I was going to be very disappointed if we were not at least pushing for success on all four fronts.

★　★　★　★　★

The first major problem to confront me as I tackled my first season as cricket manager was, inevitably, that of Boycott. Before leaving for Australia he had been given a deadline of 31 December by the county committee to decide whether he was willing to take up a two-year contract as a player, under the new captain, or whether he wanted to find a new career elsewhere. Appreciating that Geoff had problems in trying to find form as England's Test opener in Australia while, at the same time, trying to decide what his cricketing future was to be in England, the committee then extended the deadline by a month. At the very last minute Geoff cabled his acceptance of the two-year contract Yorkshire had offered him.

Making a decision like that cannot have helped Geoff in Aus-tralia, any more than his delay in making it helped us at home trying to work out our plans for the new season. But he returned to the fold, along with the other players, one week before the normal start of pre-season training and his approach to the season was entirely wholesome. As I have said, it was my intention from the start to concentrate more on the physical side of tuning up, and so I had arranged that week of exercises at Carnegie Physical Education College, in Leeds. The College, in turn, were interested in the opportunity to make tests of various kinds on cricketers because they hadn't had the chance to test them in the past. We had stamina tests, reaction tests, breathing tests – you name it, we were tested on it. After that we went to Headingley in the normal way, but instead of simply having nets in the afternoon we had more physical fitness routines every morning. The difference between what the players could accomplish physically at the end of three weeks as compared with what they could do at the start of that period was amazing. Our physiotherapist, Eric Brailsford, felt that at the end of those three weeks many of the players were up to the fitness standards of footballers – not all of us, but certainly the younger ones. Everyone really pushed himself to the limit. We were doing circuits of eighteen separate exercises – thirty seconds 'on', five seconds rest – three times through the whole routine. That is a lot of exercises: and they came after we had done half-an-hour of general stuff up and down the terraces. Afterwards there was shuttle-running to three different spots, which is generally good practice for running between the wickets.

Everyone, in fact, worked very hard indeed for an hour and a half every morning before getting out into the nets after lunch. Neil Hartley, who had been mostly involved in playing for the Colts, had been working on this sort of exercise all through the winter and he was the man who set the standards. At the beginning the gulf between him and some of our less fit players was a pretty wide one, but once they had got into the routines the gap was narrowing all the time. I felt it was a tremendously good thing that someone who was basically a second team player was the one who was doing forty press-ups a minute while Test players and established first-teamers were trying to work up from thirty to somewhere a bit closer to Neil's standards. Things were going well so far.

After Easter we got four days of good practice out in the middle, thanks to something approaching a miracle (after the weather we had had) by the new groundsman at Headingley, Keith Boyce. All the time the team spirit was developing, and as we worked up to the start of the season I felt that the spirit was as good as that of any team I have ever been involved with. It was very good to be a part of it.

The dreadful weather which marked the start of the season came as a terrible anti-climax. We had a good practice match at Worcester, and then interruptions by snow, hail and good old-fashioned rain as we tried to play a county championship match

143

with Northamptonshire at Middlesbrough, Leicestershire there in the John Player League, Nottinghamshire at Bradford in the Benson and Hedges, and then Derbyshire at Headingley in the county championship again. Three competitions, three different kinds of interruptions, and it was frustrating in the extreme because after Worcester everyone was raring to go.

I suppose one shouldn't complain when the batting got off to such a good start, but things are never perfect and when the season was three weeks old we were more than a bit rusty in the field. Because we had batted first against Northamptonshire, Nottinghamshire and Derbyshire (and not played at all against Leicestershire) the bowlers had scarcely been required to run up to the wicket. The rustiness applied to John Hampshire as well, as the new captain, because it is in the field that a captain really has to do his stuff. He needed to get used to handling the team and to moving everyone around. The bowling rate (and its accompanying clauses) is now a rather important matter, and players have got to know where they have to go at the end of each over. If they do it instinctively we are on our way to saving seconds between the overs, and at the final count-up all those seconds are going to be important.

As far as the batting was concerned, we felt fairly satisfied because basically everyone who had batted had done pretty well, and in Boycott's case, exceptionally well. When he came back from Australia I had a word with him because I felt he had got too far round in his chest-on stance and he agreed himself that he thought he had come a bit too far round. So he tried going back a bit more towards his old style and within a week or two in the nets he was playing really well. He got runs against Northamptonshire, more against Nottinghamshire (and got them in a comparatively sprightly style in a limited-overs game) and then, the following Wednesday, he scored 150 not out against Derbyshire and he really did look good.

This was very good news for me and I felt that if he could really settle down, to do his own thing simply as a player in the side and to *enjoy* his batting, then he could have as enjoyable a season as he had ever had in the game. Geoff is a loner, and I don't think anyone is ever going to change that. He always has piles of letters, and when he comes in he spends a lot of time reading them and answering them; when the team is away he usually likes to go back to the hotel and have a meal in his room or watch television, rather than get into a crowd to have a beer and a laugh. That is not a desperate thing; I believe people like that can fit into the pattern of a team if they are all right when they are with the rest of the boys. At this stage there was no cause for complaint at all; Geoff had been fine when he was with the team and the spirit was good. There had been no problems and I fervently hoped things would stay that way.

I was sorry, therefore, to see some of his supporters not only continue to exist as a group but for the group to materialise rather obviously in those early games of the season. Rightly or wrongly, there was a fair bulk of Yorkshire members who disagreed with Hampshire replacing Boycott as the captain in 1979. They staged a campaign to get that decision rescinded; they achieved their first objective in getting an extraordinary general meeting called and, on a vote by the whole membership, they were defeated. Right – they had fought their campaign, and they had given Geoff support and loyalty which must have made him very proud. But in the final vote they were defeated. That was the time to shut up shop and get down to being Yorkshire members again. The new captain now needed support, even more than Geoff had done in view of all the furore which occurred while John was away for the winter, playing in Tasmania.

In my view the 'anti' group should now have accepted that the battle was over, that Yorkshire cricket was more important than any individual or, indeed, any minority viewpoint. Its members should have given their backing to the new regime – committee (now radically changed in structure and personnel), captain (who had always been a good, loyal and popular Yorkshire player for seventeen years) and, I hoped, the manager, who was as concerned as anyone about restoring the county to the position he had grown up believing and accepting as its rightful one – at the top.

As the season began, the Reform Group were holding a dinner in Sheffield where some of the speeches did not exactly suggest that all our problems had been surmounted. During the first game at Middlesbrough there was a gathering of Geoff's personal fan club from the Reform Group. Now that might have been a perfectly innocent gathering of good, honest Yorkshire supporters and I very much hope it was. On the other hand, the winter of 1978–79 caused a tragic amount of bitterness and division in the ranks of members and supporters, and the last thing we wanted to see was any continuation of it. There was no problem from Geoff himself; he seemed to be enjoying his cricket and he was certainly playing well and that was what we all wanted to see. There was just a feeling that it wasn't going to do him any good in the long run if these cliques of his personal supporters were still grouping round him and prolonging the agony of a dispute which had caused more than enough trouble all the way round. My own view was that Geoff had a season ahead of him which would see him play more strokes than ever before and in which he would *enjoy his cricket* more than ever before, if only those no doubt well-meaning but misguided followers would leave him alone to get on with it.

I certainly didn't want problems from that quarter. Naturally, I didn't want any problems at all if they could be avoided, because life was rather hectic at the beginning of the 1979 season. First of all I began to realise just how much I was going to miss playing. When cricket has been a major part of your life for twenty-seven first-class years, it is not easy to accept that those days, basically, are over. Leicestershire had released me as a player and we had cleared the way for me to turn out with Yorkshire if it was ever necessary, or desirable. But by and large, my playing days in county cricket were over and this was what I had, first of all, to force myself to accept.

That was not going to be easy. Involvement in the first-class cricket circuit is very much more than a job of work – it is a way of life. One has friends in every county and it is always a pleasure to look forward to seeing them again. There are hotels where one has stayed, year after year, and the staff have become friends. There are restaurants and pubs which one has visited for more than a quarter of a century. There are dressing-room attendants, scorers, regular supporters at a score or more of grounds, all of whom one expects to see, renewing acquaintance, in the course of a season. Most of all there is the playing of a much-loved game on grounds one has known since teenage days – some of them with happy memories of outstanding performances, of wins against the clock, of championships won and lost, of days in the sun and days when we have watched the rain beating down or a howling gale hustling across the field.

It can never be easy for any player to contemplate retirement and that, perhaps, is why so many who do, stay on as managers, coaches, or scorers, and the rest are rarely seen on grounds once they have finished with the game. Cricketers generally are not good watchers of cricket; they have to be involved or the enchantment of the game they have loved is lost. So these were some of the thoughts going through my mind as 1979 dawned in the cricketing sense.

The committee did not want me to get involved in other aspects of the operations of the club if it was going to be at the expense of my association with the team, but in twenty-seven years I had acquired a lot of contacts as well as making a lot of friends. Perhaps now was the time to use some of those contacts. Jack Butterfield, who had run the promotions side of Yorkshire cricket, had left to join a football club and though there had been a lot of applicants for his job, they all wanted a lot of money. So before any appointment was made, and before the season began to require every minute of my time, I began to ring round and talk to a few people. Fortunately, within a few days I managed to come up with a contract with Berger Paints which was going to mean around £75,000 over a period of three years. It was a good start and it was followed by a number of other offers of sponsorship, plus a large number of promises for next year from firms which were already committed to advertising and sponsorship budgets for 1979. At the end of a few days on the telephone I felt it would be a disappointment if the club was not getting £50,000 a year from sponsorship in the next year or two. We were on our way.

19

DISAPPOINTMENT, DISENCHANTMENT AND NEW HOPES

By the last week in June, Yorkshire were near the top of the John Player League table, in the semi-final of the Benson and Hedges Cup, and had not lost a game of any kind. But in the county championship, we hadn't won one, either. The weather was, of course, responsible for a lot of drawn championship matches and washed-out fixtures in the limited-overs stuff, but to some extent the writing was on the wall as far as our bowling was concerned, especially when Chris Old was away – and he was away through the period of the World Cup. We should certainly have picked up a few more points, starting in the first three-day game against Northants at Middlesbrough where we dropped ten catches and didn't bowl particularly well. Against Derbyshire, at Headingley (where Geoff Boycott hit a splendid 150 on an imperfect wicket on which Mike Hendrick bowled extremely well) there were again encouraging signs from the batsmen, but once more the bowling was disappointing. We should have got full bowling bonus points as, indeed, we should have done against Glamorgan.

The form of Boycott was excellent. Certainly he was looking to play strokes and to gather runs more quickly than he had sometimes done in the past. There was not much wrong with our batting and I had impressed upon Geoff that he must not feel that failure by him meant total collapse. In addition, we had started to make greater use of his bowling as England were to do with considerable success once the World Cup got under way. He is an ideal type of bowler for the one-day game because, apart from the technical aspect, he is a 'mean' bowler and hates giving runs away – an attitude which was not exactly foreign to me! But Geoff's type of accurately directed in-swingers meant he could be tremendously effective in cutting down scoring-rates when he was bowling to a six-three field ... more effective than an off-spinner, for instance, because with his extra bit of pace it was difficult for a batsman to get 'inside' him. So in the one-day games our idea was to use Geoff and Bill Athey as one bowler.

In the early championship games it wasn't quite so easy, and with Geoff and Chris involved in the World Cup it became, in fact, very difficult. The crunch came at Worcester on 23, 25 and 26 June where, after scoring 393 for four, of which Jim Love hit 170 not out, we had Worcester in trouble on a pitch which had taken fifteen hours of rain over the weekend. But again, we did not bowl as well as we could have done and they avoided the follow-on, which was a disappointment. In fact Worcestershire declared with nine down, so we were left to build on a first-innings lead of 133. Once again we saw some good batting. Bill Athey got out of his sick bed to play a fine innings of 79 not out and Jackie Hampshire, who had hoped to declare at ten minutes to one on the third day, was actually able to do so ten minutes earlier than that. Worcestershire needed 329 to win in 247 minutes, or about 77 overs. To my intense disappointment, they got them with five wickets, and eight balls, to spare.

There were a number of reasons for this. After drying, the wicket rolled out into the usual easy-paced New Road track; Glenn Turner, who went on to finish with 148 not out, was dropped when he was 70; but above all we did not bowl well enough – again. You could not say that anyone bowled badly throughout, but there was no consistency in our attack. After seven or eight decent overs, one or other of the bowlers would come back and bowl badly in his next six or seven. There simply was not enough concentration by any of the bowlers. There seemed no understanding that this was simply an extension of the one-day game where a bowler is required to concentrate hard for only eight, or 11 or 12 overs, depending upon which competition it is. In championship matches the concentration has to be applied all over again when you come back – and just as hard. Of course we missed Old. There is no doubt that by this time in his career he had become a very fine bowler indeed. But his absence is not enough to explain that first defeat in any game of the 1979 season. We had a talk afterwards and I hammered home again and again my point about concentration. One accepts that it is not easy to switch so frequently from one-day games to three-day, but I pointed out to the team that they were professionals, and *Yorkshire* professionals at that, and there could be no real excuse for lack of concentration. That had to be inexcusable at any time, but when an opposition side could hit 329 to win in the fourth innings – even on a Worcester pitch – it was quite unacceptable.

There were problems before we selected the team for the next championship match at Harrogate, against Somerset. Boycott was back from the World Cup squad and one batsman had to lose his place. This was obviously a bit hard, because it was the bowlers who had not done their stuff at Worcester – but the balance of the side was the real issue. With Old back, one bowler had to step down for him and the man to go out was Graham Stevenson, a 'capped' player who had been the number one bowler at Worcester and who had finished in that second innings with figures of 18-0-80-0. Those are perhaps typical figures for Stevenson who can be an absolutely first-class bowler but who bowls too many bad balls. Perhaps the Headingley Roses match in 1978 really sums up his bowling; he had a career-best return there of eight for 65 off only 11 overs. He bowls a very good, 'unplayable', ball but in between he bowls a lot of loose ones which makes him a bit of a risk in all forms of cricket. So he became twelfth man at Harrogate and that still left the problem of which batsman to leave out.

Love had made 170 not out in the first innings at Worcester and none at all in the second innings. That sometimes happens to players. Part of it, in fact a lot of it, is psychological. A really big score in the first innings is quite often followed by a wretched one in the second. Athey had failed in Yorkshire's first innings but in the second, while still feeling ill, he had made a splendid 79 not out followed by a good 50 in a benefit match for Chris Old. I had to decide whether Love or Athey should be left out against Somerset. My reasoning was this. Athey, in my view, and that of a lot of other people, was always going to be a very good player; he had not had a good season in general because often he went in to bat when there were only a few overs left and he had been put in the position of just having to get on with it. In short, he had suffered because the openers had played too well. At Worcester he had failed in one innings and had played extremely well in the other. Looking at the temperaments of the two players, I reasoned that to drop Bill might do more harm than good. I didn't expect Jim Love to like the decision to leave him out, and in fairness to him I had already decided that if Bill didn't come off in the Somerset match, then he would have to stand down while Jim had his chance.

Already people were beginning to talk about the case of Dickie Bird and since I was in the Yorkshire side at the time I didn't really need to be reminded of it. Dickie, a Colt standing in while senior players were unavailable, scored 181 not out for Yorkshire against Glamorgan in 1959 and never played in a championship match again. He later moved to Leicestershire and after that became a first-class umpire. Here was Jimmy Love scoring 170 not out – like Bird, an 'uncapped' player – and being dropped for the next game.

The parallel was obvious and it was quite understandable that people should be starting to note it. I hoped history was not going to repeat itself, because Love was too good a player for any county to lose. One of them – Athey or Love – had to be left out of the side against Somerset, and I was the one who had to make the decision. In taking over the appointment of manager I had insisted on the right to select the first team. I had been given the power; I could not shirk the responsibility. But it wasn't easy ... I had always known it was not going to be easy.

★   ★   ★   ★   ★

On Wednesday, 4 July, the first big exodus of Yorkshire cricket-lovers to a match outside the county for a long, long time was under way from first light and even earlier. Many travelled overnight, and took a chance of getting a room in a hotel; one member I know left at four o'clock on the morning of the game eating sandwiches with his coffee en route to join the excited crowds packed into the small and (let's face it) inadequate for the occasion ground at Chelmsford.

Essex were on the very brink of their first honours. Not only had they never won a title or a trophy, they had never even been in a final. But they had gone off like a rocket in the county championship, and were now something like sixty points ahead of their nearest rivals; but all kinds of things could happen between this point and the end of the season. The Benson and Hedges Cup was the more immediate target and the semi-final is a match you have just got to win. To reach a final and lose is not a pleasant experience, but at least you have the satisfaction of having taken part in the big occasion. To go out at the next-to-last hurdle is anti-climactic in the extreme, and has been known to cause a team to go to pieces right in the middle of the season. If we lost, it was my job to see that didn't happen but as we went to the ground that Wednesday morning there could be no thought of losing. True, Essex were really on the crest of the wave. Graham Gooch was in prime form, backed up by Hardie and McEwen; Keith Fletcher had developed into a fine county captain, Denness was vastly experienced, Turner an excellent all-rounder and Lever had already swept through the batting of half the sides in the country.

Against that, Yorkshire were conditioned to winning even if this was something ingrained in the county character rather than born of recent experience. The batting had been prolific in the previous match against Somerset at Harrogate; and while our bowling was not the most devastating in the country by any means, I felt that if it was backed up by top-class fielding, it could be good enough to contain Essex's scoring within reasonable bounds. The first significant event of the day was the withdrawal from the side of Geoff Boycott with a slight strain in the leg. Nevertheless, I felt this might be a blessing in disguise in certain circumstances. It seemed that these circumstances, providentially, existed when Jackie Hampshire and Richard Lumb scored 106 with barely a third of our overs gone. I was sure this wouldn't have happened if Geoff had opened.

But his absence left the middle order short of experience and there were complaints, after the game, because Hampshire had not been available to take his usual place at number four, to steady the ship, so to speak. But if he had been at number four, I'm pretty certain the flying start would not have materialised – so that brings us back to square one. Also, one has now to start to consider the performance of 'the youngsters' in specialised batting positions. With the best possible foundation laid, with all the time in the world to establish a really good score, with just about everything in their favour, Athey, Love and Sharp managed an aggregate of just three runs. Our wonderful start was wantonly squandered by some very poor batting, by some poor shots. There was no way that we should have missed scoring 210 or something like that if we had just batted normally and sensibly, and if we had reached that score then I think we would have won the match. If Geoff had played, Jack could have batted in the middle of the youngsters and given them some steadying influence but, as I have said, if Geoff *had* opened we wouldn't have scored 106 in 20-odd overs.

We keep on saying 'youngsters', but Athey, Love and Sharp had now been playing either for one and a half or two seasons or even longer, and it was more than time that they were showing some responsibility. Everyone said, including myself, that Athey was potentially a great player but he had got to show it, especially on occasions like the one in question. The shot he played to get himself out was poor – trying to cut a straight ball with a half-bat. I could not avoid a great sense of disappointment because I had talked to these lads so much about the importance of playing straight. Hampshire and Lumb had given them a wonderful opportunity, with overs in hand, to spend a little time having a look at the bowling and building an innings. I told Bill, who is a magnificent straight driver, that I would much rather have seen him go down the pitch to Ray East and try to hit him straight for four or six. I could have accepted that, but not the stroke which got him out, or some of the others, either.

We managed to total 174 which was not enough, yet Old and Stevenson bowled so well with the new ball that, with a little bit of luck, we might still have scraped home. I have to say that everyone fielded well and the bowling basically was good considering that there was really nothing to bowl at. Even so, Essex took 54 overs to get the runs and that wasn't because they paced the innings precisely – it was because they were really made to work. Unfortunately, we hadn't quite enough runs to put them under severe pressure.

We bowled well enough during the vital stage of the innings but just when a really outstanding over was required, we would get one which gave away five or six runs. With only those 174 runs to play with, we never quite got into a position when we could play on Essex's inexperience. It means quite a lot to be used to this sort of situation so when a side is not accustomed to it there is always a chance of panic setting in. It's something we have all seen many times in one-day games, especially on the really important occasions, and if we had been able to force Essex into a position where they needed nearer 10 an over at the end, the pressure would have told.

So – we were halfway through the season, out of one of the one-day competitions, out of the race for the championship, it seemed – what was left? We were reasonably placed in the John Player League table, and it looked to me as though there were one or two sides in the middle of the table who were going to win some important matches ... teams like Leicestershire, who were beginning to find their touch, and Gloucestershire, with Zaheer and Sadiq back together. These counties had to play some of the leading sides, and I felt that some of the leaders were going to lose a few matches, so now we had to string together six or seven more wins. In the county championship, it was important to finish amongst the leading counties, and the Gillette Cup had yet to come.

*   *   *   *   *

The Gillette Cup match with Durham at Chester-le-Street caused me a bit of anxiety, again largely because we didn't bowl too well and allowed them to get 20 or 30 runs more than they should have done. Psychologically, Durham started with a couple of big advantages: as the junior county they had nothing to lose and there was that little bit of history in the background which saw them established as the first minor county to beat a championship side, in 1973 – and the side they beat were Yorkshire, at Harrogate. They were not likely to forget that, nor were Yorkshire.

So a few nerves could be forgiven. Nevertheless, as a professional I could not approach the game with defeat even as a possibility in my mind, and I didn't expect the team to think that way, either. Durham included Wasim Raja, the Pakistan all-rounder, who is a good cricketer, and Lance Cairns, the New Zealand swing-bowler who is a renowned big-hitter, as 1978 and 1979 crowds at Old Trafford will testify. As professionals in north-eastern League cricket, they played for Durham as match pros.

And Cairns it was who caused a few butterflies in the stomach towards the end of the innings. He loves to put the ball right out of the ground, and with the relatively small playing area at Chester-le-Street that was always going to be possible if we allowed him to hit the ball in the air. I felt we allowed him to do this just a little too often by not bowling a full enough length, and as a result Durham scored around 20 runs more than they should have done. It was the stand between Boycott and Hampshire which made the game safe for us; if one of those had gone early there would have been a hell of a lot of pressure on the less experienced players once again and, as we had seen, they didn't react to pressure as, perhaps, they ought to have been doing by this time. We got through and to my great disappointment, were drawn to play away yet again – this time at Lord's against Middlesex. We seemed to be meeting Middlesex more often than our next-door neighbours, and before the Gillette quarter-final we had two games against them – a Schweppes county championship match at Scarborough, with a John Player League fixture sandwiched in on the Sunday.

By now, in late July, a few restive stirrings were taking place in the ranks of the Yorkshire members. These were understandable to some extent. Yorkshire were county champions for the first time in 1867 but it was in the 1880s that the real period of consistent success began, and that continued for eighty years or so. Yorkshire were expected to win titles as of right and if the team didn't win, there were inquests throughout the length and breadth of the broad acres. With their own influential press gallery watching every game and commenting regularly on every aspect of the county's cricketing life, Yorkshire were always under keen and critical scrutiny. Only once in those eighty years had there been a period of ten years without a Yorkshire championship, and that was between 1949 (when we shared with Middlesex) and 1959, when that young side under the leadership of Ronnie Burnet started a period of spectacular and prolonged success. And while those ten years were undoubtedly lean years as far as titles were concerned, there were at least two crumbs of comfort for us. First, The Oval was tailor-made for Laker and Lock during the time Surrey were acquiring seven successive championships and everybody knew it; and second, the Yorkshire side of that period (which had to play on every kind of wicket imaginable, none of them even remotely the type that our bowlers most wanted to see) was still contributing player after player to the England side: Hutton, Lowson, Watson, Wardle, Appleyard, Trueman, Close. That was a period of frustration rather than despondency. In July 1979, Yorkshire's members had no such galaxy of international stars to gaze upon, and they were left to reflect that our last major title had been won in 1968 with a Gillette Cup victory the following year. In the fifties there had always been the possibility of success; in the seventies it seemed rather more remote.

So the new appointment had been made, Yorkshire's first cricket manager had been brought in, and the public, starved of success for so long, expected a somewhat revolutionary change in county policy to bring miraculous success. Again, I have to say I could not blame them. I could only hope that their initial enthusiasm and understandable optimism was only temporarily blinding them to all the problems which stood in the way of that instant success. I could not work miracles, and I certainly couldn't work them overnight.

The first two-thirds of that Scarborough weekend were not at all good either for the public's confidence in my appointment or their faith in the team. I accepted that having asked for, and having been given, certain responsibilities, I was bound to be in the firing-line when things went wrong. I picked the team, in consultation with the captain, and if the team performed badly then I was going to have to shoulder a good deal of the blame, at least in the eyes of the general public. I had told the players what was expected of them and I knew their capabilities – but in the last analysis, I couldn't play their cricket for them. In short, having put my confidence in them as players, my reputation was to some extent in their hands. When they did not play well on the Saturday and Sunday of that weekend, it was impossible not to feel the disappointment, bordering on disillusionment, in the ground.

In the previous county championship match at Worksop we had lost to Nottinghamshire because we did not bowl well enough in the first innings and because we dropped two vital catches. The members' confidence was balanced on a knife-edge when we went out to field against Middlesex on Saturday, 28 July at Scarborough. Now crowds at Scarborough have always been big ones in the holiday season. One month earlier, playing Somerset there, we had had a full house at a time when we had something to play for in almost every aspect of the season. Here, one month and three or four bad results later, the North Marine Road ground was packed once more and there was something touching about the loyalty of these Yorkshire supporters. At Worksop, Boycott had batted magnificently in the second innings – as well, I think, as I have ever seen him play – and David Bairstow had had a great knock only to get out to an appalling shot at exactly the wrong time. If those two had gone on until lunchtime the game against Nottinghamshire would have been saved but – and it's very hard to say but it has got to be said – one bad shot lost us the position which those two had worked so hard to establish. That was what we had got to eliminate: elementary mistakes which cost us so much. So many times we had done the wrong thing at the wrong time, and if we were to have any sort of future at all it had got to stop. Unfortunately it didn't stop at Scarborough, at least not on the first two days. On the third, we batted well to win the Schweppes match but by then a lot of damage had been done and we had put ourselves out of the running in the John Player League.

On the Sunday in particular, some of our work was unbelievably bad. While we had put down a number of vital catches during the season I had felt that the all-round work in the field was generally good and I hadn't seen many sides perform better. But at Scarborough there was some mis-fielding on the ground and some untidy throwing to the wicket. It was doubly unfortunate that another full house saw this, when very few Yorkshire supporters had been present as the lads performed infinitely better on grounds further afield: but there it was, and the shortcomings were fully exposed. The bowling was poor and the batting was bad, on a perfectly good wicket. To rub it in, during that week both John Lyon and Bob Ratcliffe had made maiden centuries for Lancashire at Old Trafford. All right – it was against Warwickshire, with quite the worst attack in the country, but hundreds are not easily made against anyone. Here *we* were, with all our recognised batsmen, struggling to make fifties. It was as difficult to explain as it was to digest. We had injury problems, especially amongst the faster bowlers, and Chris Old was now going to be away at the Lord's Test. Only once during the season had I been able to select from the full available strength of the county, but that wasn't the whole story. Somehow I had got to make the younger players hate defeat in the way Yorkshire teams of old hated it; I had to inspire in them that fierce, burning pride in playing for their county – and winning for it – that I had been brought up to believe in.

I was intensely disappointed with the results so far. I had not yet reached a state of disillusionment by any means, but I was baffled about what to do to put things right. Looking at things with absolute honesty, I felt the captain had lost a bit of confidence in his bowlers and that, in turn, might be rubbing off on them. What we needed was a match in which everyone did something well to restore belief in himself. Kevin Sharp, for instance – no one tried harder than him, but he was badly in need of a good score to re-establish his faith in his own ability, so I decided to give him a game in the second team to see if he could get runs. John (Hampshire) himself had had a poor fortnight as far as runs were concerned, and with everyone struggling together it was not easy for anyone to get out of the rut.

As far as team spirit was concerned, I had no worries at all. It was still a happy and harmonious dressing-room and possibly some members felt that *this* was wrong . . . that after a sub-standard performance on the field, the players should not be laughing and joking *off* it. This did not worry me. If we had had problems off duty amongst lads who were struggling to find form, then I would have been concerned, but I was satisfied that there was no apathy. The team were as concerned, and as puzzled, about the way things had gone wrong as I was and the last thing I wanted was for them to be going round with long faces and feeling sorry for themselves. Now we had to see what August brought . . .

★   ★   ★   ★   ★

As if to emphasise the inconsistency of our performances (this time in the happiest possible way however), we pulled off a spectacular win over Middlesex in the county championship match at Scarborough by virtue of some brilliant batting on the final day. Off we went to Sheffield to beat Warwickshire by 10 wickets, and things were looking distinctly better. It wasn't an easy wicket to bat on but by hard work and, this time, the right sort of application at the right time, we managed to get 259 and even without interference from the weather we thought that was a winning score. But it rained overnight and we bowled Warwickshire out for 35. They batted better in following on, as the pitch eased a bit, but we still needed only 32 to win at the end of the day. Because of the possibility of more bad weather we tried to make sure by knocking off the runs in the couple of overs which were possible at the end of the day and scored 30. I felt the last ball of the day was a wide, and if that had been given we would have wanted one to win with one ball to come. It wasn't given, and everybody had to turn up next morning for the ceremonial scoring of two runs. Mercifully, it stayed fine, and we had started to climb back up the table.

Against Leicestershire at Bradford we played on a pitch which had been covered for forty-eight hours and only exposed at ten o'clock that morning. When the grass had been cut, it did not look particularly green, but knowing that it had been covered for a full two days we also knew that whoever batted was going to struggle. Nevertheless, with uncertain weather about in a weekend game, we had to bat and struggle we did, all morning. Not many sides have four specialist seamers but with Ken Higgs, Les Taylor, Paddy Clift and Ken Shuttleworth, Leicestershire had, and they bowled well. In one way I couldn't help a feeling of satisfaction at just how well they did bowl. I thought, 'At least some of the gospel I have been preaching for the past ten years has been absorbed', as all four of them bowled a good line with an on-side field of long leg, mid-on and one man in the bat-pad position. We worked our way to 211 for eight in 100 overs; the rain which was forecast did not come and Leicestershire reached 317 for seven. Instead, the rain came at precisely the wrong time for us, and if the final day's play had not been washed out we might have been in a bit of trouble.

At least that gave us plenty of time to drive to London for the Gillette Cup quarter-final against the now-very-familiar Middlesex boys. Even the wicket was familiar – I think we had played on it ourselves once or twice! We had a long look at it as we walked across for nets at half-past nine, and we could see it 'giving' a bit under the roller. There was certainly a bit of moisture in it but when we came back, just over an hour later, it had changed completely. The top was rather caked and it looked the sort of pitch on which I would have liked to have the Leicestershire bowling line-up of the previous season – four specialist seamers, with myself and John Steele as spinners.

Unfortunately, Yorkshire's spinners had not been bowling particularly well in recent games. We had Phil Carrick with us in the party but Hampshire was not very happy with his recent performances and I think 'Fergie' would have been the first to admit that his form wasn't very good. So, having decided to play five seam bowlers and no spinner there was very little alternative to putting Middlesex in and hoping there was, after all, still a bit of moisture in the pitch to help us bowl them out for a manageable total. In the event the wicket played quite well and Middlesex scored over 200, leaving me to reflect that we would have been better off with spinners in the side and taking the chance to bat first. As things turned out, there was no way we could have won after Middlesex had batted first – because with the weather playing a major part, we went out to bat no fewer than seven times. Especially in a limited-overs match, it is quite impossible to expect a team to bat solidly and well with seven starts. So we were out of another competition, and the outlook for the success for which I had so fervently hoped in my first season of management was decidedly bleak.

Rather soberly we embarked on our three-match tour of the west and south, starting at Cheltenham, where we did as well as we could have expected in another rain-affected match, taking three bonus points for bowling and four for batting. Mike Procter slipped out the early batsmen but we went from 50 for five to 303 for eight declared, largely due to a century by Carrick. At Canterbury we had a good wicket, bright sunshine and clear blue skies, and we badly wanted to win the toss that we lost.

By this time, apart from the shortcomings of our spin attack, we were struggling a bit for seamers with Chris Old bowling off his Sunday League run; and the captain put down a couple of catches at slip. I think it was always going to be a 300 wicket, but missed catches, plus the shortcomings of our pace attack, meant that Kent got 345 for the loss of only two wickets so there were no bowling bonus points. We made a terrible start, losing our first wicket overnight. Next morning Athey had a hook at one down the leg side, got a tickle and was caught and then, in a monumental foul-up, Hampshire and Lumb found themselves both at the same end and we had three men out for nothing. On came 'Deadly' Underwood to take six for 71, and we struggled all the way to 224 all out. Kent declared their second innings leaving us to get nearly 300 on a wicket which was turning; any side in the world would be in trouble against 'Deadly' when that happens. Only twenty-five minutes play was possible on the last day, and the writing was on the wall with us at 14 for two. We had taken only five Kent wickets while they scored 515 runs; we had lost 12 wickets making a total of 238. Not a good performance. It also included a leg-side stumping by Bairstow off Old, but that was not as impressive as it sounded to people who were not at the game in view of the pace at which 'Chilly' was bowling. Quite a good stumping, but not very quick bowling!

At Hove we started by not bowling very well, and Sussex got off to a real flyer – 60 off the first 10 overs. However, Geoff Cope bowled exceptionally well (six for 30 off as many overs) and we contained them to 267. Next morning we were hoping for a 300-plus score on a good wicket when a sea-fret, of the type we often get at Scarborough, came in and hung about the ground. Leading the Sussex attack was one of the best bowlers in the country for such conditions, Geoff Arnold, and we were bowled out for 198. Once the weather had cleared up Cope made 40 and Steve Oldham a maiden 50, to indicate that without that damp mist we would have got the 300. It rained overnight, we got caught on a sticky dog and Giles Cheatle bowled us out for 110. Twice in one game we had caught the wrong end of the weather, but I have to add that we did not play particularly good cricket and I couldn't help reflecting that it was here that we had started our run of success just twenty years earlier.

Our defeat meant that it was now going to be very difficult to make fourth place in the Schweppes County Championship, and thus get into the prize money. I was disappointed, and while there had been no complaint from the committee I knew that quite obviously they were disappointed, too. We had started off so well and in that first month I felt sure that we could win something. Since then our performances had been bedevilled by an inexplicable inconsistency – and it was inexplicable. We never knew who was going to bowl badly at any given time so we could not even say to ourselves, 'So-and-so is having a bad time; we'll leave him out for a game'. If we left out one who had played badly in the previous game, it was odds-on that somebody else, who had been included, would then play badly himself. We had men who were even inconsistent in their more indifferent performances. To coin a phrase, the only consistent thing was the inconsistency.

The only comfort I could draw from the season at this stage was that I at least had a better understanding of the players' temperaments than I had when I started. Some, for instance, were very much up-and-down – either on top of the world or wholly dispirited. In the next season I had got to make them understand: 'Don't be so "high" when you are winning, and don't be so "low" when you are losing.' I had got to get that straightened out with two or three players to get them more evenly balanced, and if that didn't work, then I would have to face the fact that some of our players weren't good enough. In August 1979, I did not believe that was the case and I did not want to have to believe it.

David Bairstow and Graham Stevenson in particular were either right up or right down. Arnie Sidebottom was another who could become very depressed, although basically he was a fighter and I believed his fighting spirit would, eventually, make him a good cricketer. Chris Old ... well, his attitude is pretty well-known throughout the game. He hasn't the heart to bowl quick when he has even slight muscle-trouble. I know, we all know, that there are certain injuries which will always prevent one bowling, but I don't think 'Chilly' has ever been prepared in his life to grit his teeth and say, 'I know I'm feeling twinges but the side needs me to bowl well and quickly in this situation so I'll do it'. We have missed this quality from Old because there have been so many times when we have needed him badly. Fit, and bowling well, he is a very fine player. I just wish he had more heart.

Life was not made any easier at this stage by dark mutterings off stage. One story brought to me was that the group of members who had tried so hard to have Boycott reinstated as captain were now saying: 'We didn't get Hampshire out, but we will get Illy out.' The original Boycott supporters were now calling themselves the Yorkshire Members' Action Group and there was talk of them forming themselves into a Supporters' Club. If that was their idea, I was all for it because the club, and the players, would always welcome support. But to stand in the background and niggle could do no good at all. We had a group of these people with us on the southern tour and one or two of the players got them in a bar one evening and gave them a right ear-bashing which I hoped might help to get them thinking on the right lines. Support we welcomed; sabotage we could well do without.

The season ended on a much happier, more successful and (from the point of view of the county's future) highly encouraging note, not simply because in our last two matches we beat the ancient enemy in the Headingley Roses Match and then the 1979 champions, Essex, at Scarborough. What delighted me most of all was the confidence, the maturity and the responsibility shown by another young player who was not really one of those mentioned as our 'white hopes' when the season began.

Neil Hartley, at twenty-three captain of Bingley in the Bradford League, had played one match for the county in 1978, scoring 30 runs against Derbyshire at Sheffield and earning himself a one-line entry in *World of Cricket*: 'Sound young Yorkshire batsman.' We had reintroduced him in 1979, but against Leicestershire at Bradford he had lacerated an arm rather badly chasing a ball to the boundary and he wasn't ready again until Lancashire came to Leeds for the traditional match. It was a 'struggle' match for the most part and the wicket, though brown in appearance, turned out to help the seamers for most of the game. I thought we played fairly well. Boycott got his usual quota of runs; everyone did his bit in winkling them out, but they hung about in the second innings to the point where I was just saying, 'Well, that's it. There isn't time for us to win now', when the last wicket fell. I honestly didn't think there was a reasonable chance of our winning because there were only 14 of the last 20 overs remaining when we went in needing 104 to win. In normal circumstances, seven an over is a tough target and, looking rationally at the way we had been playing, I could not see anything more than a draw as the result.

We got the runs in 13·5 overs largely because of a quite magnificent innings by Hartley. Nothing – nothing at all – which had happened during the season delighted me and encouraged me more than the way Neil played. It was not just that he stroked the ball superbly, but he ran just as intelligently as he ran athletically between the wickets. He knew how many balls had been bowled, where he wanted to be, where to place his shots – it was an innings of astonishing maturity. Psychologically it was good for the whole team, because apart from Neil's example they could reflect that they had won without Geoff Boycott, who took no part in the second innings.

Hartley will be twenty-four when the new season starts. He has had to wait around for his chance for a few years although his ability has been well-known in the League. He bowls a bit of medium pace and is a splendid field because he is a physical fitness fanatic, playing rugby and generally keeping himself in trim all the year round. In the Roses Match he gave me exactly what I had been looking for in a young player all season – concentration when it was most required, an awareness of all aspects of the situation, doing exactly what was wanted *when* it was wanted. We had two or three young players capable of playing this type of innings, but this was the first time one of them had done it. I was absolutely delighted.

So it was on to Scarborough for the last championship match and there we found an ideal cricket wicket. If the sky had been overcast I think each side would have been bowled out for about 100, but with clear weather the ball came on to the bat so that everyone could play shots. Yet there was enough grass on the wicket to encourage the seamers, and it turned a bit towards the end – the perfect wicket for a good game of cricket over three days, and the sort I remember with affection from my own playing days at Scarborough. Both sides scored over 300 in the first innings, we bowled Essex out for 150-odd in the second, and we won well into the last 20 overs with our last pair at the wicket – the perfect match!

I couldn't help feeling that if we got more wickets like that we would win more matches than we lost, and the crowds would see some excellent cricket. We had taken on the champions and beaten them, and we had done it without Boycott who had returned, injured, from the final Test at The Oval. Neil Hartley played another good knock, Richard Lumb batted well as he had done all season, and we had Chris Old looking a little bit more like an England fast bowler. Arnie Sidebottom bowled magnificently throughout the match, and showed that if there is a bit of something in the pitch he can use it. Right at the death, we had Graham Stevenson playing a very responsible knock as he had done three or four times during the season. That is exactly what I had been looking for, especially from players like Stevenson, so once again I felt greatly lifted by the whole team's performance.

We wound up the season with a John Player League match at Edgbaston. Here we had conditions where the ball swung so much that it frightened some of the less experienced bowlers. Old, on the other hand, used them to bowl quite beautifully – he got two for 13 in his eight overs, and he could easily have had four. But Stevenson, fresh from the maturity he had shown as a batsman at Scarborough, now seemed a bit naive as a bowler. Because it was swinging so much, he was sending down a couple of off-side wides and then, in trying to counter the swing, bowling one down the leg side. This was daft. It was like me getting on a big turner – you pray for conditions like that. And here we had a young bowler who could and did swing the ball a lot, being overawed because it swung too much! Young bowlers have just got to learn to harness this sort of advantage, and turn it to their own benefit. It doesn't take a lot of working out to decide to use the whole width of the bowling crease when there is excessive movement either in the air, or off the pitch.

So Warwickshire made 177, which was quite a few more than they ought to have done in those conditions. And, after fielding a depleted attack for most of the season, they were now better equipped with Willis, Rouse and Perryman all playing. We got ourselves into a position where we needed about seven an over in the last 10, and Neil Hartley came in to play another absolutely magnificent innings. You can tell how well he played when you see that he got 50 out of 70-odd, with John Hampshire in full cry at the other end.

As at Headingley, Hartley played an innings which no overseas star could have surpassed – Clive Lloyd or anybody else. It was superb. If a schoolmaster finds all the drudgery of his job (and there can be a lot of drudgery) worthwhile with the emergence of just one academically-gifted pupil, I was left feeling that the disappointments of 1979 – and I had experienced many of those – were perhaps just a little more bearable after three glimpses of Neil Hartley as my first season in management came to an end. A new year, 1980, was ahead. There was a lot of work to do. But at least I knew that the potential was really there.

Nevertheless, the winter of 1979–80 was not a time to sit back and reflect that there was real talent in the pipeline to develop. We had to take positive action to make sure that the latent ability in the Wesley Street Schools and the Farsley juniors of the 1980s was going to be developed. We called a meeting of the major Leagues of Yorkshire just before Christmas to put a number of points to officials which we felt would help to channel that ability towards the county side. I had played a few Bradford League games for Farsley during the 1979 season, and I had been distressed by what seemed to have happened to the game – it had gone defensive to an alarming extent. What I wanted to see was not merely the abolition of the pernicious limited-overs form of cricket, but a much more positive attitude adopted by bowlers, batsmen and, in particular, captains. I wanted to see the side batting first allowed to bat as long as the captain wanted, but the points-system for drawn games changed to encourage him to exercise judgement about when to declare. I wanted to see the captain then decide how much time he needed to bowl out the opposition and to provide his bowlers with attacking fields which would test everybody – for bowlers to concentrate on line and length, for batsmen to cope with an all-out attack and yet to chase the runs needed, for fieldsmen to be one hundred per cent on their toes all the time, and for captains to work out field-placings which had real significance, to handle the bowling changes well and to understand the strengths and weaknesses of the batsmen. In short, I wanted them to play cricket.

The Leagues listened to what we had to say, and went back to report to their constituent clubs. Another meeting was fixed for the new year. It may take time, perhaps a couple of seasons, to get everyone thinking in a positive way. There will be arguments and no doubt some disagreements. But I draw confidence from the one common factor in all our discussions – we are unanimously determined to make Yorkshire cricket great again.

20

THE CIRCUS COMES TO TOWN

If the finances of first-class cricket had been on a better-organised footing, there would probably never have been any Packer cricket at all. Granted, Kerry Packer wanted his own way in the televising of cricket in Australia and, as we saw, he was prepared to go to pretty extreme lengths to get that, certainly as far as money was concerned. But in England at any rate there was no great enthusiasm for his circus. There is simply no substitute for the atmosphere of an England–Australia Test.

One can see why West Indian and Pakistan players supported him pretty strongly because, modest as the rewards were in England, they were certainly better than those offered in other overseas countries where it is impossible to think of cricket as a full-time career. And, to be fair, once he had started his circus Mr Packer provided a few interesting innovations. By far the most successful of these was floodlit cricket; but while I can understand the novelty of this having an appeal in Australia, in the West Indies and South Africa, for instance, it is, nevertheless, rather difficult to imagine a crowd sitting watching at ten o'clock at night at Bradford, or Derby, or Northampton, even in the balmiest English summer. His promotion of the game, too, gave orthodox cricket something to think about – do we do enough to publicise our Test cricket and to sell it to the public? On the other hand, would the game lose much of its natural dignity if it were the subject of the ballyhoo which accompanied the World Series matches in Australia and on their tours? We are confronted with the two extremes of cricket thinking – on the one hand, the almost futuristic presentation of the game served up by World Series, and on the other, the feudalistic stranglehold which Lord's still exercises despite all the reorganisation and reconstitution which has been taking place. Let no one forget that it was not Lord's which went out and discovered that there was money in commerce and industry which could be made available for cricket sponsorship: it took a man outside the game to do that.

So, financially, the game needed shaking up – there is no doubt about that. Mr Packer started by paying his players well, but let us not hail him as a new Messiah for that. He simply took the cream from the top. He had none of the expense of finding and coaching young players to become world class; he did not have to provide facilities and staff to groom new talent; he did not have to provide grants to scores of organisations involved in cricket development.

Mr Packer simply flashed his cheque book, and a very large proportion of the best players in the world went running to him. He contributed nothing to the development of the future of cricket in the world, and in Australia he went a very long way towards destroying it utterly. If Australia had won the Fourth Test in Sydney, in January 1979, as Australia most certainly should have done, then it might have been a different story altogether. That would have levelled the series at two-all and there would have been everything to play for. The Australian cricket public, already fired by the win in the Third Test in Melbourne by a young side, virtually without international experience, would, I am sure, have flocked to watch the deciding matches of the series. The England team included exciting young players like David Gower and Ian Botham, and there was always that very epitome of Pommie opposition, Geoff Boycott, struggling to find form. The Aussies love nothing better than a Pommie cricketer to hate; they had a ready-made one in traditional terms whenever Boycott went to the crease; and they found a new anti-hero in Botham, whose aggression and natural belligerence got them going from the very beginning.

When Botham took a wicket, bowling from the pavilion end in Sydney, and raced down the pitch giving the V-sign to the frenzied multitudes on The Hill, his friends trembled for him. When Rodney Hogg, Australia's new fast bowling folk hero, sank to his knees with the effort of unleashing an extra special thunderbolt, Botham's taunt was audible not only to the Aussie fieldsmen but to some of the crowd as well: 'I know I'm great, Rod, but you don't have to worship me in public.' Botham doesn't accept the existence of physical danger; he doesn't understand the meaning of fear. If Australia could just have kept up that wonderful come-back which started in Melbourne and continued in the first innings in Sydney, we could have had a series to remember. Packer would have been left for dead. His counter-attraction was based on a publicity campaign which invited the public to watch the world's fastest bowlers in action against the world's greatest batsmen, and on paper that was true.

But what is the point of gathering together a group of the world's greatest batsmen when you have a battery of the world's fastest bowlers banging in four, five and six short-pitched deliveries an over? The only stroke open to batsmen is a hook, so no wonder the circus carried around with it, in an extensive entourage, its own doctors! If one talked to the World Series batsmen individually and off the record, there was more than a little disillusionment with the nursing of cut heads and broken noses. But publicly they maintained a closed-ranks loyalty to the cause: their contracts were pretty specific.

The television-viewing public cannot have derived much pleasure from the series with advertisements coming up at the end of every over and the fall of every wicket, with caption-ads flickering across the foot of the screen as well, even as the ball was being bowled. A friend of mine watched an hour and a half of it with a stop-watch in his hand and the advertisements appeared every two minutes fifty-five seconds! Can you imagine a British audience, reared on the best and cheapest television in the world, standing much of that?

So a win by Australia in the Fourth Test at Sydney could have changed the whole face of cricket's greatest controversy. Sadly, Australia not only lost but lost badly – lost after being in an almost unassailable position, lost because of dropped catches and immature batting technique against good, but not unplayable, spin bowling. Australians don't like to lose and particularly they don't like to lose badly. Their attitude is perhaps best summed up by the plaintive bleating of one of their commentators, as Brearley packed his on-side fieldsmen for a double off-spin attack by Miller and Emburey: 'Well, if England are going to play it like this they are not going to encourage the Australian batsmen to go for their strokes.' Have you ever heard such a naive comment? Strokes? They hadn't got any strokes. They hadn't got any kind of operating technique against that sort of attack, which was sad for Australian cricket.

In a marvellous climate like Australia's, with a wealth of sporting facilities – natural and created – there are many alternative attractions when things are not going well in one particular sport ... tennis, golf, swimming, surfing, and simply the beach. With Australian cricket on its knees, the public were not going to watch the *coup de grâce*; they were going off to find something more appealing to their patriotic instincts. This was not necessarily Packer cricket – because not many people watched it apart from a couple of floodlit evenings.

But the damage had already been done when Mr Packer creamed off all the best and most experienced players in Australia. The Chappells, McCosker, Hookes and Marsh would certainly not have allowed Miller and Emburey and Brearley to dictate so completely the way they played in the Fourth Test. What Packer did for Australian Test cricket was to destroy it; what he did for English cricket – mercifully, but without seeking in any way to do so – was quite the reverse. We could cope with the loss of our Packer pilgrims, those signed up by Tony Greig as he, sadly, abused his position of captain of England. We absorbed the loss of Amiss, Woolmer, Underwood, Knott and Snow without any undue problems and, in fact, their departure hastened the development of players like Gower and Botham, Emburey and Edmonds, and it gave Bob Taylor the chance for which he had waited so patiently. And how magnificently he took that chance.

Even more important, Packer pushed the English cricket authorities into realistic Test match fees more quickly than had been intended. They had been talking about £700 a match when Packer came on the scene and, with the help of sponsorship from the Cornhill Insurance Company, this was now increased to £1,000 per man per Test. At last Test cricket had moved into the 1970s. Before the Tests became the Cornhill Tests, it is by no means certain that fees would have gone beyond £700: indeed, I am not even sure they would have *reached* £700.

However, once Test fees had reached a realistic figure I then became a bit concerned about the way wages were developing in the game as a whole. My view was that at £1,000 for a Test, those fees should remain stable for a while until the pay for rank-and-file county professionals had a chance of catching up, *pro rata*. I talked to a number of England players and, to be absolutely fair to them, they agreed that before Test fees were increased again (to £1,200) some of the money which had become available should have gone to county players. I genuinely believed that the top players were now getting enough money to ensure that they stayed in orthodox and established cricket; the time had come to try to ensure that county players got an extra £1,000 or so a year on top of their normal wages.

That brings us to the subject of differentials. When I first played with Yorkshire all capped players were paid the same amount, and I felt that we gained more from that than the county, or individual players, would have gained from some being paid more than others. Times have changed, attitudes have changed, degrees of ability have changed. The one thing that hasn't changed is Yorkshire's insistence on players being native-born Yorkshiremen and that is something I don't think one single member would want to see changed. Everyone else imports players from overseas; we think – as we have always thought – that there is enough native talent to make and to keep Yorkshire cricket great.

But, as I say, times have changed and we now have differentials within Yorkshire despite having no 'immigrants'. One, which I don't think anyone will complain about, is that players get extra money for every two years of service as a capped player so that someone who has done ten years now gets £500 or £600 more than someone who has just started. I think all members, today, will accept that. Apart from that, I personally do not think, today, it is a particularly good thing to have differentials within a county side. This is one advantage of being manager of a Yorkshire side. Where you have players from overseas who have had to be *bought* from their own countries, you are obviously going to have other players with mixed feelings. By and large, the imported stars have done their stuff and individual counties would be the poorer without them; but from time to time you find one import who does not deliver the goods, and then you are bound to have resentment from players (on half the import's stipend) who must ask, 'Why are we paying him all this money?'. Once that happens, team spirit is starting to go down the drain. Just take a look at what happened to Lancashire in the two seasons after Colin Croft joined them.

Returning, for a moment, to Packer, and more particularly to the way English players were recruited, it must have been the best-kept secret in the history of cricket in this country. There is a pretty good grapevine in the game and I always thought I was reasonably close to it, but I had never even heard a whisper of Greig's recruiting campaign until it broke in the newspapers. I don't blame Greig for trying to further his own career. I have always got on well with him and I quite like him as a person. But I am bound to agree with the general feeling throughout the game that it was not quite 'on' to use his position as England captain to negotiate with players on behalf of another boss. Like a lot of my fellow professionals, I was disappointed with Greig's lack of integrity. If he had openly announced his new allegiance and invited people to join, then I don't think there would have been much ground for complaint. Shock there would certainly have been, because the whole concept of Packer came as a shock to established cricket – but at least we would all have been spared the distaste which was generally felt when the story so unexpectedly broke.

The Cricketers' Association attitude to the whole Packer situation was, I believed, reasonable in the extreme. The chairman, David Brown, and the secretary, Jack Bannister, felt as I did, I think – that you cannot serve two masters. Test cricket as administered by the International Cricket Conference, and by World Series Cricket under the auspices of Mr Packer, were two entirely different things which, at times, were going to be in direct opposition to each other. Players had to decide which of the two masters they wished to serve. The members of the association, I believe, did not accept that money was essentially the deciding factor. There were members who felt very strongly anti-Packer, especially those who toured Pakistan in 1977–78 and were faced with the possibility of playing a Test match against Packer imports who had been flown back from Australia especially for the Third Test in Karachi. They won their particular battle with the Pakistan authorities after a good deal of telephoning between Pakistan and Lord's, but they came home with very strong views on the subject. Fortunately for cricket as a whole, an attitude of sweet reasonableness won the day when the Cricketers' Association met in England after that tour – but we were still left with one or two rather militant resolutions on the table in the hope that ICC would sort the whole position out during the following year.

The ICC is supposed to be the overall governing body of world cricket and the time has come – no, it is overdue – for it to make decisions which are binding on all its constituent members. It is simply not good enough for member countries to go back home and say (or be told) that certain decisions are not acceptable and that individual countries are still going to go their own way.

From what I have heard from Tony Greig and one or two other people, the Packer regime considered asking me to join the World Series. In the end, I understand, it was decided that probably I was a bit too old and that was fair comment. So I was never put in the position of having to make a decision about whether I could go and join that form of cricket. All I can say about that is that if someone had offered me £20,000-odd for three seasons it would have had to be very seriously considered.

What I can say, and what I have always said, is that I did not for one moment blame the lads who did go to Australia and play in the World Series. I said, right from the start, 'Good luck to them'. But what I also said was that they could not have their cake and eat it. World Series cricket in Australia was like someone opening a brand-new, streamlined, chromium-plated business in the same street as an old-established business of the same type – not necessarily selling a better product, but very definitely constituting serious trading opposition to the original business. Once our players had joined the opposition, they couldn't expect to be welcomed back into the English Test side while that opposition was still operating.

However, by the summer of 1979, it seemed that some sort of agreement was reached between the TCCB and the Packer organisation, because Australian cricket was virtually bankrupt and Packer now had the franchise to televise its Tests. No one – or at least very few people – seemed to know exactly what that agreement was, but if it involved Packer's English players being recalled to our Test side then, in my view, we had to say, 'so be it'. The bright new business down the street was no longer in opposition to the old-established firm; we were all now on the same side with, no doubt, the old firm due to be given a rather brighter and more modern image. Mr Packer's organisation were now its marketing managers in Australia and we had to expect something of a facelift.

Whether that would necessarily be a good thing, or whether it would please everyone in the game elsewhere in the world (or even in Australia itself), was something we would have to wait and see. But *if* there was a satisfactory agreement, and *if* we accepted that we were now all on the same side, and *if*, of course, the players in question were good enough on current form, then I couldn't, at the end of 1979, see that there was a strong case for excluding them.

At the same time I hope posterity will give the credit which is due to the Cricketers' Association for the part it played in the whole Packer affair. If it had not been for the Association's threat to ban Packer's men from English county cricket, I don't think there would have been any compromise agreement reached at all. I attended meetings with David Brown and Jack Bannister at which I got a very distinct impression from the MCC representatives – Charles Palmer, David Clark and F. G. Mann – that they had no bargaining power with Packer apart from the more militant resolutions of the Cricketers' Association which had been left 'lying on the table' for a year to see if any progress towards a compromise agreement was made.

The Cricketers' Association stand had been the one strong aspect of English participation in negotiations with Packer. I think it is fair to say that about threequarters of the members of the association, from the first, wanted compromise but certainly not peace at any price. When England agreed to undertake the 1979–80 tour of Australia, it seemed that that compromise had been achieved. I wasn't sure of all its terms; I didn't meet anybody during the season who *was* sure just what all the implications were. But at least the World Series games were not going to be staged in direct opposition to orthodox Test cricket in Australia, and therefore the agreement seemed to me to open the door for the return to our Test sides of the Packer men.

There were predictable rumblings from the current players but there had to be two ways of looking at this. All right – the 1979 series players had stepped in to fill the gaps left by the Packer men and their Test record over two winters and two summers was a good one. But leaving aside for the moment the opposition during that period (which is, of course, highly relevant if you look simply at results and evaluate them) let's take, for a moment, the other view: the 1979 players had got their places *because* Underwood, Amiss, Woolmer and Knott had gone to Packer. And they had come in just at the moment when playing Test cricket for England had started to mean big money. Knott, Underwood and company had given great service to England over a long period, for peanuts. Underwood had 272 Test wickets ... Knott 252 wicket-keeping victims and 4,385 Test runs ... Amiss 3,736 Test runs. For a long and difficult tour of Australia in 1970–71 the pay was £1,500. In 1979 almost that amount could be picked up for one Test match.

Because the Packer men signed contracts for three years and the series was called off after two, Underwood was lucky enough to get two pay packets while playing for England on the tour and again I said, 'Good luck to him'. It was sheer luck that things turned out that way; it was not greed which put him in the position of being paid twice.

My view, as the party was picked for the 1979–80 tour, was that the England players should stop complaining and get on with playing cricket. They were being very well paid for doing a job they ought to enjoy.

When the Packer organisation ultimately were awarded the contract to televise cricket for the next three years there seemed to be a fair number of strings attached. His marketing organisation were to package and promote the game and most of those with experience of the way the World Series had been 'packaged and promoted' heard the news with foreboding. India, who were due to tour Australia during the winter of 1979–80, appeared joyfully and happily to stand down at the first suggestion of their doing so and West Indies and England, with their superior drawing-power, were asked to stage a three-cornered competition of one-day internationals with Australia as well as each playing three orthodox Tests against the host country. A bit of lobbying had been going on!

There was a lot of heart-searching at Lord's before it was agreed that England would go. It was clear that ICC help was essential to bail out Australian cricket from the financial mess which had been created the previous winter, but at the same time there was a natural revulsion in England from debasing the currency of orthodox Tests with Australia which had been gilt-edged for more than a hundred years. The proposed itinerary was complex and ex-hausting. The deliberations were not helped by what seemed a rather modest guarantee offered by the Australian Board of Control, especially when it was related to demands by the England players for yet more money. (Somehow or other that was very quietly swept under the carpet but not, I am quite sure, before at least part of their demands had been satisfied. We seemed to be approaching a position where a player who gets into an England Test side at twenty and stays there is going to be in a position to retire at twenty-five!)

Nevertheless, I think it was right for England to take part. The Australian finances were in such a state that they had to have help to get something back in the coffers and because England–Australia Tests have always been the *crème de la crème* of Test cricket we not only had a moral obligation to help, instincts of self-preservation also demanded that we give it. But once we were there I was rather disappointed to get a distinct impression (view-ing and listening and reading at a distance of twelve thousand miles) that Packer's merry men were running things to a greater extent than we had been led to believe would be the case.

I don't think it did much for cricket to see our players decked out in black pads and the other paraphernalia of floodlit cricket – I'm afraid they looked rather like clowns and that isn't really the impression you want to plant in the minds of spectators or televiewers. And the crowds, I think, were disappointing. When I saw England playing Australia in Sydney (and on Boxing Day, too, when the biggest crowds were to be expected) before twenty-nine thousand people, I recalled that in 1971, after a washed-out Test in Melbourne we played a hastily-arranged one-day match before forty-four thousand – and they came despite the absence of packaging and promotion!

There can be no doubt that the Australian public have been saturated with cricket now for three consecutive winters and not all of it the sort of cricket with which I would want to be associated. Also, in two of those winters, England have been heavily involved out there and the delights of Pom-bashing are coming round a little too regularly to retain their fascination for the Australian public. I fervently hope that as the Packer contract expires the Australian Board of Control will, in fact, get back control and that aluminium bats, coloured shirts and large-scale histrionics will be buried for ever. I cannot see Packer starting up his circus all over again if he doesn't get a chance to prolong the cynical mockery he has made of a wonderful game, and we had better pray pretty hard that he doesn't. The damage that he has done to international cricket has been devastating but not quite irreparable – yet.

21

MY HOPES FOR
THE EIGHTIES

My two most earnest wishes for the 1980s are to see Yorkshire back as a power and force in English cricket and to see South Africa back in Test cricket.

The first is an obvious choice but not essentially a selfish one. I have enough Yorkshire arrogance to assert that the game needs a powerful White Rose team challenging every year for the championship title. The drawing-power of teams in the seventies was based more on the spectacular ability of their overseas players than the all-round strength of the counties themselves ... Viv Richards and Barry Richards, Clive Lloyd, Mike Procter, Andy Roberts, Zaheer Abbas, Wayne Daniel, Alvin Kallicharran, Bishen Bedi, Imran Khan, Eddie Barlow. Every county has had its imports except Yorkshire. It used to be every county's delight to beat Yorkshire; it used to be the beneficiary's first choice for his match. The Yorkshire match was the one that brought in bigger crowds because the supporters, no less than the players them- selves, wanted to see those cocky northerners beaten. Everybody played just that little bit harder when the opposition wore caps bearing a white rose.

That reaction was a tribute to my county, and Yorkshire players accepted without complaint that they were made to work and fight harder than others. We had come to expect it over more than a century of striving to be nothing less than the best. Through the seventies, sadly, the kudos attached to beating Yorkshire has steadily declined to a point where, finally, it means no more than beating any side, and less than beating the reigning champions, or the Gillette Cup-holders, or the Benson and Hedges winners. That has got to change. Counties must once again find that beating Yorkshire is the hardest task of all and thus one to relish above all victories. Yorkshire pride, which has taken a ten-year battering, must be restored. We need it; cricket needs it.

Test cricket needs South Africa, too. India and Pakistan, and also New Zealand, have improved their standards a great deal in the last ten years but they still haven't the drawing-power of Australia and West Indies. As we have seen, some of the mystique and magic of Tests against Australia has been dissipated in the past three years, which leaves us with the West Indies as almost the solitary top attraction.

So in terms of variety in the Test calendar and attractiveness in the opposition, cricket needs South Africa back in Test cricket. I was saddened and disappointed when she was excluded in the first place because it meant another triumph of the politicians over the sportsmen. This is something I regard, in its own way, as being as reprehensible as one country's interference in the domestic affairs of another's. There is no problem with the players. South Africans have played alongside West Indians and Pakistanis and Indians regularly in the English County Championship; John Shepherd and Younis Ahmed have been in sides which have toured South Africa and there has been no problem.

South Africans have been amongst the most admired players in English county sides during the seventies with no problems. South African golfers regularly compete on the British tournament circuit; indeed, one of them, Gary Player, is one of the most respected golfers in the history of the game. South African tennis players compete at Wimbledon and in provincial tournaments, and there is no problem. South African rugby tourists have been and gone without any major difficulty, despite the deafening sabre-rattling and blood-curdling threats of major disruption which preceded their visit. Why, then, is Test cricket singled out as the one area where spectators are deprived of the chance to see some of the fine players who have remained unseen for the past fifteen years? It is said that disruption would be inevitable because cricket is vulnerable to that highly vocal .001 per cent of the population who always seem to be able to have their views expressed in newspapers, and on television and radio, in total disproportion to the 99.999 of the rest of us. But is a Test match ground more vulnerable than a championship golf course?

The South African cricket authorities were asked to achieve

greater integration of black and Cape coloured players and they did it. Still they are not welcomed back to the fold. The Rugby Board of Control were asked to do something similar and they did it. And when they came to pick a multi-racial team to visit England the new outcry was, 'Oh but you don't really mean it. You've only picked some black and coloured players as a bit of window-dressing'. What the hell *do* these people want?

I think they want permanent estrangement in cricket because it provides the perfect political stick with which to beat South Africa. Most cricketers, I am absolutely certain, want South Africa back; the vast majority of the cricket public, I am equally certain, want South Africa back. And cricket itself *needs* South Africa back. My wish for the 1980s is that we shall see her players on Test grounds again.

Beyond those matters (which I suppose might be described as being at the higher levels of policy) I return to an old hobby-horse of mine – creating greater interest in county championship cricket by giving it a face-lift. Promotion and relegation are absolutely vital, in my view, in order to achieve this. There are signs of some interest in this direction by adding Scotland to the 1980 Benson and Hedges tournament (with D. B. Close at the helm!) and it may be that Scotland would be interested in becoming the eighteenth 'county', so to speak, to make up two divisions of eight clubs. An alternative would be to combine two minor counties – Norfolk and Suffolk, Cheshire and Staffordshire, or Cornwall and Devon are possible combinations which come to mind.

I have said these things before, to many people and in many places, and I suppose there is a possibility of leaving myself open to the suggestion that it is Illy singing the same old song. But because I learned at a very early stage of my life to appreciate the value of money, there is nothing I hate more than to see it being wasted, or at any rate to see opportunities to make money being disregarded.

Cricket needs money. It is an expensive game to organise, to administer and to stage. If you just think of the value of city centre sites in terms of land and buildings, and then consider the fragmentary use which is made of them during the course of a year, you begin to get an inkling of how much money is involved.

Cricket cannot continue to exist as we have known it (and, indeed, as we have come to know it more recently) without frequent and substantial infusions of income. So when the opportunities are there before us, it horrifies me to see them being wasted. Sponsorship, it has been established, is available but can we rely on its being available indefinitely? Is it enough for us simply to say, 'Oh well, if one firm pulls out next year we have two or three on the waiting list'? I insist that we must look around at every possible way of making our game more attractive so that it brings in more spectators in its own right. Then, and only then, can we reasonably expect sponsors to want to put money into cricket at the same time as we are creating more wealth ourselves. The simplest and surest way to do this is to provide a more competitive spectacle.

When the draw for the 1979 Benson and Hedges semi-finals was announced and we were faced with a trip to Chelmsford, I went on record as saying it was a pity that such games were not staged on neutral grounds. I was not saying anything I had not said before – many times – and I was not complaining that Yorkshire had to face a game a long, long way from home. Partisanship amongst cricket spectators does not have the same effect on a visiting side as it does, say, on a football team having to go to Old Trafford or Anfield, or an international rugby fifteen to Cardiff Arms Park.

There are certain fringe advantages like knowing conditions on your home wicket, but by and large most experienced players know what to expect when visiting most of the other grounds in the country. Home advantage in a county cricket match is not a completely vital factor. But from the moment the draw was announced the office staff at Headingley were inundated with calls for tickets. Within a week we had more applications than there were tickets available. So much for those who say supporters will not travel long distances, especially in mid-week. To look at it from the Essex standpoint, naturally enough they were pleased to be at home, but when they had to go to Taunton in the 1978 Gillette Cup semi-final they took with them a huge and enthusiastic following despite the distance and despite the fact that this, too, was a Wednesday match. So why not stage semi-finals on neutral grounds which will accommodate a bigger attendance than the average county ground? I would have liked to see the Essex v Yorkshire tie staged at Leicester, not for sentimental or personal reasons but because I know that Grace Road can stage the big occasion and stage it well and because I know perfectly well we would have had twice or three times the 'gate' which could squeeze into Chelmsford. I believe there would have been fifteen thousand at Leicester. We could get – what? – five thousand into Chelmsford. We would have had twenty thousand if it had been played at Headingley, but that is the luck of the draw. What I am saying is that when it comes to raising money the game so badly needs, it should not be a matter of luck but of sound economic planning. I have said it before and I shall continue to say it: cricket just cannot afford to throw away income which is there for the taking.

The same applies to the county championship. It is the real essence of cricket, the competition which means far more to players – and, I believe, to the people who really care about cricket – than any other, but for years it has been ailing. When we get to the last few weeks of the season and there is a keen contest for the title, then we see the crowds. They come flocking to watch the three-day game. So why not give them keen competition for most of the season?

If we had two divisions with two-up and two-down promotion and relegation, the supporters of virtually every county would be involved in some form of fiercely competitive cricket throughout the season. Soccer has discovered (and, let's face it, that has not always been the most imaginative sport when it comes to moving with the times) that a fight to avoid relegation will inspire at least some form of enthusiasm amongst spectators. Anything is better than having two-thirds or even more of our sides simply fulfilling fixtures for a large part of their summer.

I put this point to the TCCB some years ago and got a good hearing. I thought we had a good chance of seeing two divisions come into existence, but when the idea got as far as county committees, through their chairmen, I think the fear was of losing important traditional fixtures like, for instance, the Roses match. The 1979 Roses match at Old Trafford lasted for just one hour; play during the remainder of the three days was completely washed out so Lancashire were going to have to do without their best home fixture until 1980 anyway. That is always likely to happen.

In English weather, looking forward to one particular game as the major money-spinner is nothing better than a lottery, so I don't see how that argument can really stand up. Fixtures in a two-division contest would ensure home and away games against each county in one's own division, giving that particular contest a more realistic look than we have at present. And the fixtures would be more easily manageable to avoid clashes with Tests. It would be possible to stage seven-eighths of the county matches so that they were clear of Tests, and I would always want to see the first three days of Test matches completely clear of county fixture opposition. To me there is a simple logic to all this, and it saddens me to think that the opposition to the idea cannot be based on sound economic commonsense.

What I really cannot stand is the determination of some influential members of cricket's hierarchy in their steadfast refusal to move with the times. I am not, and never have been, wildly revolutionary in my ideas. I love my cricket as much as anyone who has ever been connected with the game, and I have never wanted to see change simply for the sake of change. But it has got to be accepted that time does not stand still in any context.

Just as the technique of players today is vastly different from that used in the twenties and even thirties, so their philosophy is different too. Their personal financial circumstances are different. Equally, we have a different kind of spectator. Whether the traditionalists like it or not, the noisy boisterous crowd is here to stay, even at Lord's. One might almost say especially at Lord's, thinking of Gillette and Benson and Hedges Cup finals. And after the miserable start to 1979 with match after match washed out, wasn't it marvellous to experience the atmosphere at Lord's in the opening game of the World Cup between England and Australia? This is the atmosphere 'instant' cricket has created, and while we might think it is a far cry from the genteel dignity of Tests before the war, we have not merely to tolerate it but we have to encourage and stimulate it.

As late as the early sixties we used to have amongst Yorkshire's more devoted followers a group of schoolmasters who, as soon as the long summer holiday released them from the classroom, went on tour with the county side. Their hotels were booked year after year and we used to exchange a friendly smile in the bar at the end of a day's play because they were just as much a part of the Yorkshire scene as we were. They are no longer seen at Scarborough and Bournemouth and Dover and Clacton. I like to think that this is due to a passage of time rather a change of tastes, but whatever the reason their absence is a sign of the changing times. Sad though this may be, nevertheless it has to be accepted. No new group of schoolmasters has replaced that one.

The end of season Festivals have all but disappeared, and Scarborough is not the same as it used to be. But Scarborough still exists as a Festival and its organisers for years have been making a real effort to adjust to a different pattern of life, and family holidays, and what the public want. Harrogate has even emerged as an innovator, with a mid-season mini-Festival.

However, some things *don't* change and mercifully one of them is the deep, sentimental affection that English people have for the game of cricket. While that remains we still have something to build on. In the smaller towns and villages of Yorkshire there are still people who have never seen a first-class cricketer in action, except 'on the box', yet they still wait for the arrival of the evening paper, or listen to the news, to see how the team has fared that day.

I found such people in Leicestershire, too, and I like to think they exist in all other counties. We have to find out what they want and we have to give it to them. I believe the best, the most attractive thing we can give them, is competition. Sport today has to have point and purpose. Teams have to have an objective and motivation. Traditions are important because they are the foundation on which the game has been built, and I think that cricket has managed to retain most of the best of them. But, in themselves, they are not enough as we enter the 1980s. The emotional and traditional roots of the game are secure; we have to cultivate them using modern methods. We have to plan with the tastes of the 1980s spectator in mind. The last two decades have shown us the direction in which we have to go; we can't stop now.

A few final words about the future. One thing I am particularly anxious *not* to see in the eighties is any increase in bad manners by players on the field, or any more irresponsible behaviour by spectators. In fact I very badly want to see that eliminated altogether. True cricket-lovers do not misbehave. But just as the game needs television, not only to bring the game into more homes but to attract greater sponsorship as well, so it has to contend with those infantile imitators who are the curse of association football. They see one or two louts and idiots indulging in exhibitionism, and they cannot resist trying it out themselves. This, combined with the attractions of licensing law relaxations, add up to a serious danger to the civilised conduct of county cricket. Noisy and boisterous crowds are here to stay; they do not have to be ill-mannered and undisciplined crowds.

Mercifully, we have not yet reached the stage when many players set a bad example to the crowd in the way that this happens in some other games, but it is beginning to creep in to a degree which must give rise to some concern. I do not like, and never have liked, ostentatious indications of disagreement with umpires. The captain has the means of making a team's views known about matters which are likely to be the subject of dispute and it should be left to him to do it. Equally, a captain has a responsibility to the game, as well as his players, by curbing exhibitions of over-enthusiasm as well as dissent. And at the top playing levels of the game I am more than a little concerned about the greedy, I'm-all-right-Jack, attitude which has crept in recently. Certainly players have needed to be paid more for a long time now, and certainly a constant watch has to be kept on wage-scales to see that they do not fall again below acceptable levels. But it is more than time that some attention was given to the rank-and-file county player in this respect. The Test men have got their rewards, and very handsome rewards they are too; now it is time that more serious consideration was given to the bread-and-butter cricketers who are never going to get into a Test side, but who do an invaluable job for their counties year in and year out.

Summing everything up, I want to see South Africa back in Test cricket; Yorkshire back in their rightful place; an imaginative, forward-looking concept of county championship cricket, with two divisions and promotion and relegation; less ill-mannered behaviour and near-hooliganism in our grounds; a more generous attitude by counties (and by cricketers in more exalted areas of the game) to colleagues who miss out on high Test match fees and all the fringe benefits, of which there are many.

In the hope that the 1980s will see some of my ideals fulfilled, let me end on an optimistic note by looking at a brighter future in the form of some of our more promising young players. Look out for:

Batsmen (and here I think Yorkshire are more fortunately placed than many counties) – Bill Athey, Jim Love, Kevin Sharp, Neil Hartley, Nigel Briers (Leicestershire), Dipak Patel (Worcestershire), Paul Parker (Sussex).
Bowlers – Graham Dilley (Kent), Jon Agnew (Leicestershire), David Gurr (Somerset), and Nick Cook (Leicestershire).
Wicket-keeper – Jack Richards (Surrey).

The eighties can be good for cricket. Everyone in the game has a part to play to make it the most significant decade in the history of the game.

APPENDIX:
CAREER RECORD
1951-1978

Compiled by Roy D. Wilkinson

Debut for Yorkshire: *v* Hampshire at Leeds, 18 August, 1951
Debut for Leicestershire: *v* Cambridge University at Cambridge, 3 May, 1969 **Captain** 1969–1978
Debut for England: *v* New Zealand at Manchester, 24 July, 1958 **Captain** 1969–1973

Season	M	Inns	NO	Runs	HS	Avge	100s	50s	Overs	Mds	Runs	Wkts	Avge	5 in Inns	10 in Mtch	Ct
1951	1	1	0	56	56	56.00	0	1								
1952	6	6	2	152	48	38.00	0	0	101	26	227	7	32.42	0	0	2
1953	34	40	11	823	146*	28.37	1	2	813.2	241	2023	75	26.97	2	0	11
1954	24	33	5	426	59	15.21	0	2	309.3	93	683	25	27.32	1	1	14
1955	28	36	6	1040	138	34.66	2	5	591	198	1358	48	28.29	0	0	24
1956	34	46	8	755	78	19.86	0	4	620.4	204	1348	103	13.08	5	1	12
1957	33	52	9	1213	97	28.20	0	8	831.2	289	1951	106	18.40	7	1	17
1958	32	46	9	643	81*	17.37	0	2	717.2	224	1621	92	17.61	7	0	12
1959	33	50	13	1726	162	46.64	5	5	1041.1	340	2361	110	21.46	3	0	30
1959–60 (WI)	12	16	2	353	100	25.21	1	2	365	107	781	11	71.00	0	0	3
1960	33	49	10	1006	86	25.79	0	4	992.3	422	1914	109	17.55	7	1	25
1960–61 (SA)	4	6	2	83	31	20.75	0	0	86	23	240	5	48.00	0	0	3
1961	34	51	4	1153	75	24.53	0	8	1104.3	437	2292	128	17.90	9	1	25
1962	36	56	9	1612	127	34.29	3	8	1081.2	426	2276	117	19.45	8	0	28
1962–63 (Aus.)	8	12	3	248	65*	27.55	0	2	†186.5	35	611	12	50.91	0	0	5
1962–63 (NZ)	4	4	0	81	46	20.25	0	0	50	21	98	5	19.60	0	0	5
1963	22	31	5	676	107*	26.00	1	0	483.4	171	1078	60	17.96	4	0	15
1964	33	44	9	1301	135	37.17	2	7	1012.2	374	2131	122	17.46	7	1	17
1965	32	47	8	916	90	23.48	0	3	854	360	1630	98	16.63	6	0	25
1966	27	39	8	673	98*	21.70	0	2	830.1	316	1680	100	16.80	8	1	22
1967	27	36	9	759	68*	28.11	0	4	880.3	365	1613	101	15.97	6	2	8
1968	31	37	9	819	100*	29.25	1	3	957.2	360	1882	131	14.36	7	2	16
1969	25	37	10	950	153*	35.18	2	4	599.1	206	1186	62	19.12	2	0	11
1970	23	38	4	1047	102*	30.79	1	6	539.1	155	1261	47	26.82	1	0	7
1970–71 (Aus.)	12	18	4	479	53	34.21	0	1	†243	59	781	20	39.05	0	0	4
1970–71 (NZ)	2	3	0	58	36	19.33	0	0	†41	12	102	0	—	0	0	2
1971	22	30	5	682	107	27.28	1	3	633	230	1269	64	19.82	3	0	15
1972	17	26	6	538	57	26.90	0	3	376.3	105	778	39	19.94	0	0	9
1973	17	25	3	670	79*	30.45	0	4	474.4	143	1044	28	37.32	1	0	5
1974	21	27	8	448	67	23.57	0	2	535.1	204	1014	57	17.78	4	0	7
1975	21	33	11	997	88	45.31	0	6	459.1	158	1068	51	20.94	2	0	21
1976	23	37	7	879	135	29.30	1	4	389.2	143	772	36	21.44	1	0	16
1977	25	24	3	506	119*	24.09	1	1	388.4	144	777	37	21.00	1	0	11
1978	17	15	2	209	39*	20.90	0	0	261.4	86	635	25	25.40	2	0	5
Totals	753	1051	207	23977	162	28.40	22	106	†470.5 / 18379.1	6677	40485	2031	19.93	104	11	432

† 8 ball overs

OVERSEAS TOURS

1959–60   MCC to West Indies
1960–61   Commonwealth Team to South Africa
1962–63   MCC to Australia and New Zealand
1970–71   MCC to Australia and New Zealand

CENTURIES (22)

For Yorkshire (14)

v Essex	146* at Hull, 1953
	116 at Southend, 1955
	150 at Colchester, 1959
v Hampshire	115 at Bournemouth, 1962
v Kent	135 at Dover, 1964
v Leicestershire	100* at Sheffield, 1968
v Surrey	127 at The Oval, 1962
v Sussex	122 at Hove, 1959
v Warwickshire	107 at Sheffield, 1962
	107* at Birmingham, 1963
v Indians	162 at Sheffield, 1962
v MCC	138 at Scarborough, 1955
	105* at Scarborough, 1959
	103 at Scarborough, 1964

For Leicestershire (4)

v Essex	153* at Leicester, 1969
v Glamorgan	102* at Leicester, 1970
v Northamptonshire	119* at Leicester, 1977
v Nottinghamshire	135 at Leicester, 1976

For England (2)

v India	107 at Manchester, 1971
v West Indies	113 at Lord's, 1969

For Players (1)

v Gentlemen	100 at Lord's, 1959

For MCC (1)

v Berbice	100 at Blairmont, 1959–60

TEN WICKETS IN A MATCH (11)

For Yorkshire (11)

v Glamorgan at Swansea, 1960	15 for 123 (8 for 70 and 7 for 53)
v Gloucestershire at Harrogate, 1967	14 for 64 (7 for 58 and 7 for 6)
v Hampshire at Bournemouth, 1961	12 for 102 (7 for 39 and 5 for 63)
v Kent at Dover, 1964	14 for 101 (7 for 49 and 7 for 52)
v Leicestershire at Leicester, 1966	11 for 126 (5 for 96 and 6 for 30)
at Leicester, 1967	11 for 79 (6 for 52 and 5 for 27)
v Surrey at The Oval, 1954	10 for 110 (2 for 41 and 8 for 69)
v Warwickshire at Middlesbrough, 1968	10 for 71 (4 for 27 and 6 for 44)
v Worcestershire at Bradford, 1956	10 for 62 (4 for 36 and 6 for 26)
at Worcester, 1957	12 for 91 (3 for 49 and 9 for 42)
at Sheffield, 1968	10 for 79 (6 for 42 and 4 for 37)

NINE WICKETS IN AN INNINGS (1)

For Yorkshire (1)

9 for 42	v Worcestershire at Worcester, 1957

EIGHT WICKETS IN AN INNINGS (5)

For Yorkshire (4)

8 for 70 (1st inns)	v Glamorgan at Swansea, 1960
8 for 50	v Lancashire at Manchester, 1961
8 for 69	v Surrey at The Oval, 1954
8 for 20	v Worcestershire at Leeds, 1965

For Leicestershire (1)

8 for 38	v Glamorgan at Swansea, 1976

SEVEN WICKETS IN AN INNINGS (17)

For Yorkshire (13)

7 for 49	v Essex at Middlesbrough, 1958
7 for 53	v Glamorgan at Swansea, 1960
7 for 58 (1st Inn's) } 7 for 6 (2nd Inns) }	v Gloucestershire at Harrogate, 1967
7 for 22	v Hampshire at Bournemouth, 1953
7 for 39	v Hampshire at Bournemouth, 1961
7 for 49 (1st Inns) } 7 for 52 (2nd Inns) }	v Kent at Dover, 1964
7 for 40	v Northamptonshire at Northampton, 1962
7 for 89	v Nottinghamshire at Scarborough, 1964
7 for 62	v Surrey at The Oval, 1964
7 for 54	v Warwickshire at Middlesbrough, 1961
7 for 73	v MCC at Scarborough, 1968

For Leicestershire (2)

7 for 18	v Nottinghamshire at Leicester, 1974
7 for 27	v Warwickshire at Leicester, 1969

For An England XI (2)

7 for 51	v Young England XI at Scarborough, 1963
7 for 18	v England Under 25 XI at Scarborough, 1971

HAT-TRICK (1)

For Leicestershire v Surrey at The Oval, 1975

CENTURY AND FOURTEEN WICKETS IN A MATCH

135 and 14 for 101 (7 for 49 and 7 for 52) for Yorkshire v Kent at Dover, 1964

CENTURY PARTNERSHIPS

Ray has shared in 59 century partnerships – 2 for the second wicket, 13 for the fourth, 16 for the fifth, 16 for the sixth, 5 for the seventh, 6 for the eighth and 1 for the tenth. Brian Close was his partner in 9 of these stands, Vic Wilson in 5, Chris Balderstone in 4 and John Hampshire, Roger Tolchard, Willie Watson and Norman Yardley in 3 each.
    The highest stand was 228 for the tenth wicket with Ken Higgs v Northamptonshire at Leicester in 1977. They came together with 9 wickets down for 45 and took the score to 273 before Higgs was run out for 98; Ray was left not out having scored 119. This is the record partnership for the tenth Leicestershire wicket.

APPENDIX: CAREER RECORD 1951–1978

FOR YORKSHIRE
COUNTY CHAMPIONSHIP

	M	Inns	NO	Runs	HS	Avge	100s	50s	Overs	Mdns	Runs	Wkts	Avge	5 in Inns	10 in Mtch	Ct
Derbyshire	27	36	5	861	80	27.77	0	3	673.1	254	1373	60	22.88	1	0	15
Essex	21	32	9	1000	150	43.47	3	3	546.3	186	1150	57	20.17	3	0	18
Glamorgan	20	30	7	465	80*	20.21	0	2	645.1	256	1305	90	14.50	6	1	12
Gloucestershire	27	40	7	1006	98*	30.48	0	5	715.5	269	1404	111	12.64	6	1	17
Hampshire	22	35	5	692	115	23.06	1	2	479.5	185	924	65	14.21	5	1	11
Kent	20	24	5	630	135	33.15	1	3	551.3	174	1292	76	17.00	7	1	18
Lancashire	28	37	7	725	74	24.16	0	4	674.5	266	1303	63	20.68	4	0	17
Leicestershire	22	27	6	929	100*	44.23	1	7	717.4	260	1318	95	13.87	9	2	8
Middlesex	25	38	6	608	69	19.00	0	1	663.3	266	1330	70	19.00	3	0	16
Northamptonshire	20	31	6	637	70	25.48	0	3	616.3	256	1217	65	18.72	3	0	13
Nottinghamshire	27	35	10	682	94	27.28	0	4	661.5	251	1379	63	21.88	4	0	23
Somerset	24	26	4	740	98	33.63	0	5	472	157	1089	52	20.94	2	0	10
Surrey	27	45	10	666	127	19.02	1	2	808.5	252	1885	91	20.71	4	1	17
Sussex	20	30	6	738	122	30.75	1	3	452.2	177	948	45	21.06	2	0	14
Warwickshire	31	41	13	994	107*	35.50	2	4	714	283	1517	82	18.50	6	1	16
Worcestershire	20	27	4	617	58	26.82	0	3	643.4	267	1170	80	14.62	5	3	7
Totals	381	534	110	11990	150	28.27	10	54	10037.1	3759	20604	1165	17.68	70	11	232

OTHER MATCHES

	M	Inns	NO	Runs	HS	Avge	100s	50s	Overs	Mdns	Runs	Wkts	Avge	5 in Inns	10 in Mtch	Ct
Australians	7	9	2	258	69*	36.85	0	2	171	52	392	17	23.05	0	0	2
Cambridge Univ.	12	15	3	375	66	28.84	0	3	215	96	362	30	12.06	2	0	5
Canadians	1	2	0	35	18	17.50	0	0	11.3	2	34	2	17.00	0	0	0
Combined Services	1	2	1	65	56	65.00	0	1	13	3	36	0	—	0	0	1
Hampshire	1	1	0	56	56	56.00	0	1	40	9	162	4	40.50	0	0	1
Indians	3	4	0	232	162	58.00	1	0	47.3	16	93	5	18.60	0	0	3
Lancashire	2	3	0	64	49	21.46	0	0	48.2	10	126	4	31.50	0	0	3
MCC	29	47	6	1243	138	30.31	3	3	716	193	2062	85	24.25	4	0	9
New Zealanders	2	2	0	49	29	24.50	0	0	46.5	20	104	5	20.80	0	0	1
Oxford Univ.	9	6	1	113	44*	22.60	0	0	217.3	85	439	23	19.08	1	0	4
Pakistanis	3	4	1	44	25	14.66	0	0	86	38	176	7	25.14	0	0	2
Rest of England	2	4	0	116	37	29.00	0	0	62	11	206	9	22.88	0	0	2
Scotland	3	3	0	78	75	26.00	0	1	62	26	90	16	5.62	1	0	1
South Africans	3	5	0	48	17	9.60	0	0	80.2	29	198	12	16.50	1	0	3
West Indians	3	5	1	63	28*	15.75	0	0	69	22	184	6	30.66	0	0	2
Totals	81	112	15	2839	162	29.26	4	12	1886	612	4664	225	20.72	9	0	39
All matches for Yorkshire	462	646	125	14829	162	28.46	14	66	11923.1	4371	25268	1390	18.17	79	11	271

FOR LEICESTERSHIRE
COUNTY CHAMPIONSHIP

	M	Inns	NO	Runs	HS	Avge	100s	50s	Overs	Mdns	Runs	Wkts	Avge	5 in Inns	10 in Mtch	Ct
Derbyshire	14	21	5	332	65	20.75	0	1	347.3	120	649	37	17.54	3	0	10
Essex	15	18	3	630	153*	42.00	1	1	342	101	724	35	20.68	1	0	6
Glamorgan	9	10	3	270	102*	38.57	1	0	148.4	60	329	18	18.27	1	0	5
Gloucestershire	8	15	5	274	48	27.40	0	0	244.5	90	505	23	21.95	1	0	7
Hampshire	10	14	1	359	57	27.61	0	3	269.1	75	599	28	21.39	0	0	5
Kent	12	20	5	351	79*	23.40	0	1	174	48	432	11	39.27	0	0	5
Lancashire	8	11	2	166	51*	18.44	0	1	133.1	34	350	12	29.16	1	0	0
Middlesex	9	12	1	185	55	16.81	0	1	180.1	47	413	19	21.73	0	0	2
Northamptonshire	13	14	6	463	119*	57.87	1	2	240.4	90	448	30	14.93	2	0	10
Nottinghamshire	14	15	5	354	135	35.40	1	0	261.2	96	511	35	14.60	2	0	5
Somerset	7	14	3	317	67*	28.81	0	2	133	50	282	10	28.20	0	0	4
Surrey	5	6	2	134	56*	33.50	0	1	75.3	27	156	11	14.18	0	0	2
Sussex	10	13	3	392	79	39.20	0	4	302.3	133	545	27	20.18	1	0	10
Warwickshire	10	14	2	146	29	12.16	0	0	208.1	75	387	26	14.88	1	0	1
Worcestershire	6	9	3	216	88	36.00	0	2	91	25	237	11	21.54	1	0	2
Yorkshire	7	9	1	168	51	21.00	0	1	147.4	42	369	16	23.06	0	0	3
Totals	157	215	50	4757	153*	28.83	4	20	3299.2	1113	6936	349	19.87	14	0	77

FOR LEICESTERSHIRE (cont.)
OTHER MATCHES

	M	Inns	NO	Runs	HS	Avge	100s	50s	Overs	Mdns	Runs	Wkts	Avge	5 in Inns	10 in Mtch	Ct
Australians	3	4	0	68	34	17.00	0	0	51	5	163	4	40.75	0	0	0
Indians	1	2	1	84	42*	84.00	0	0	9	5	7	0	—	0	0	0
New Zealanders	1	1	1	63	63*	—	0	1	12	1	36	0	—	0	0	0
Pakistanis	1	1	0	15	15	15.00	0	0								0
West Indians	2	3	2	35	17	35.00	0	0	49	13	127	0	—	0	0	1
Cambridge Univ.	7	7	1	263	73	43.83	0	2	149	73	198	15	13.20	0	0	2
MCC	1	1	0	20	20	20.00	0	0								0
Oxford University	3	3	1	36	31*	18.00	0	0	49	22	80	4	20.00	0	0	4
Totals	19	22	6	584	67	36.50	0	3	319	119	611	23	26.56	0	0	7
All matches for Leicestershire	176	237	56	5341	153*	29.50	4	23	3618.2	1232	7547	372	20.28	14	0	84

TEST CRICKET

	M	Inns	NO	Runs	HS	Avge	100s	50s	Overs	Mdns	Runs	Wkts	Avge	5 in Inns	10 in Mtch	Ct
England v.									†172							
Australia	18	28	3	663	57	26.52	0	2	326.5	180	1094	34	32.17	1	0	16
India	8	12	2	321	107	32.10	1	1	357	144	592	31	19.09	2	0	11
New Zealand	13	16	1	320	65	21.33	0	2	†41 294.3	127	597	22	27.13	0	0	10
Pakistan	5	7	1	82	45	13.66	0	0	167	75	301	10	30.10	0	0	0
South Africa	4	6	2	81	37	20.25	0	0	77	32	146	6	24.33	0	0	1
West Indies	13	21	2	369	113	19.42	1	0	480.4	156	1077	19	56.68	0	0	7
Totals	61	90	11	1836	113	23.24	2	5	†213 1703	714	3807	122	31.20	3	0	45

† 8-ball overs

SUMMARY

	M	Inns	NO	Runs	HS	Avge	100s	50s	Overs	Mdns	Runs	Wkts	Avge	5 in Inns	10 in Mtch	Ct
For Yorkshire	462	646	125	14829	162	28.46	14	66	11923.1	4371	25268	1390	18.17	79	11	271
For Leicestershire	176	237	56	5341	153*	29.50	4	23	3618.2	1232	7547	372	20.28	14	0	84
For England	61	90	11	1836	113	23.24	2	5	†213 1703	714	3807	122	31.20	3	0	45
For Other Teams	54	78	15	1971	100	31.28	2	12	†257.5 1134.4	360	3863	147	26.27	8	0	32
Totals	753	1051	207	23977	162	28.40	22	106	†470.5 18379.1	6677	40485	2031	19.93	104	11	432

† 8 ball overs

GROUNDS IN YORKSHIRE

	M	Inns	NO	Runs	HS	Avge	100s	50s	Overs	Mdns	Runs	Wkts	Avge	5 in Inns	10 in Mtch	Ct
Bradford	51	67	14	1333	80	25.15	0	7	978	338	2329	110	21.17	4	1	31
Harrogate	14	16	5	525	89	47.72	0	4	430.3	161	905	58	15.60	4	1	8
Huddersfield	3	3	0	47	23	15.66	0	0	35	13	81	0	—	0	0	0
Hull	18	25	5	648	146*	32.40	1	4	491.1	188	906	56	16.17	5	0	11
Leeds	50	67	10	1614	97	28.31	0	11	1379.2	560	2721	146	18.63	8	0	31
Middlesbrough	16	21	4	546	84*	32.11	0	5	389.1	132	859	67	12.82	4	1	11
Scarborough	50	76	17	1904	138	32.27	3	5	1328.3	408	3448	184	18.73	14	0	19
Bramall Lane, Sheffield	53	79	17	1771	162	28.56	3	4	1377.1	544	2626	148	17.74	6	1	32
Totals	255	354	72	8388	162	29.74	7	40	6408.5	2344	13875	769	18.04	45	4	143

APPENDIX: CAREER RECORD 1951–1978

IN LEICESTERSHIRE

	M	Inns	NO	Runs	HS	Avge	100s	50s	Overs	Mdns	Runs	Wkts	Avge	5 in Inns	10 in Mtch	Ct
Leicester	100	129	38	3377	153*	37.10	4	16	2501	831	5153	254	20.28	16	2	50

OTHER GROUNDS IN UK

	M	Inns	NO	Runs	HS	Avge	100s	50	Overs	Mdns	Runs	Wkts	Avge	5 in Inns	10 in Mtch	Ct
Bath	3	5	0	47	17	9.40	0	0	41	17	96	4	24.00	0	0	0
Birmingham	25	33	6	637	107*	23.59	1	2	714.4	271	1485	63	23.57	1	0	14
Blackpool	2	4	1	167	66	55.66	0	2	42	12	129	6	21.50	0	0	0
Bournemouth	9	14	1	361	115	27.76	1	1	327.1	114	653	54	12.09	4	1	4
Bristol	12	19	6	491	98*	37.76	0	3	362.2	119	786	40	19.65	2	0	5
Imperial Cricket Ground, Bristol	1	1	0	36	36	36.00	0	0	15	7	37	0	—	0	0	1
Burton-on-Trent	1	2	0	10	10	5.00	0	0	6	4	12	0	—	0	0	0
Cambridge	18	21	4	632	73	34.93	0	5	364	169	560	45	12.44	2	0	7
Canterbury	3	4	1	7	5	2.33	0	0	66	19	149	5	29.80	0	0	3
Arms Park, Cardiff	5	9	1	227	80*	28.37	0	1	148.1	46	385	18	21.33	1	0	5
Sophia Gardens, Cardiff	2	3	0	44	37	12.33	0	0	50	23	85	2	42.50	0	0	1
Chelmsford	4	6	1	140	41	28.00	0	0	108	25	268	12	22.33	0	0	3
Cheltenham	1	2	0	74	70	37.00	0	1	38	11	81	6	13.50	0	0	1
Chesterfield	17	25	4	569	65*	27.09	0	2	457.2	184	856	40	21.40	0	0	9
Clacton	1	2	0	21	21	10.50	0	0	25	9	52	3	17.33	0	0	1
Colchester	4	4	0	261	150	65.25	1	0	85	21	237	12	19.75	1	0	4
Colwyn Bay	1	2	0	10	6	5.00	0	0	0	3	16	0	—	0	0	0
Coventry	2	3	0	24	12	8.00	0	0	8	1	40	2	20.00	0	0	0
Dartford	1	2	0	40	37	20.00	0	0	7	2	27	0	—	0	0	0
Derby	3	5	2	60	25*	20.00	0	0	61.1	16	149	3	49.66	0	0	1
Dover	4	5	1	221	135	55.25	1	0	178.3	58	383	35	10.94	4	1	4
Eastbourne	2	4	1	86	43*	28.66	0	0	47	21	108	4	27.00	0	0	4
Folkestone	2	4	1	116	79*	38.66	0	1	23	0	77	2	38.50	0	0	0
Gillingham	1	2	0	45	35	22.50	0	0	45	15	109	3	36.33	0	0	2
Glasgow	1	1	0	3	3	3.00	0	0	7	2	13	0	—	0	0	0
Gloucester	2	3	0	54	40	18.00	0	0	53	22	77	5	15.40	0	0	2
Gravesend	1	1	0	43	43	43.00	0	0	24	8	52	6	8.66	0	0	1
Hastings	1	2	0	25	13	12.50	0	0	5	0	21	0	—	0	0	0
Hove	11	15	3	519	122	43.25	1	4	297.2	119	634	30	21.13	1	0	9
Kidderminster	2	2	1	30	22*	30.00	0	0	71	32	121	5	24.20	0	0	0
Leyton	3	5	1	114	44	28.50	0	0	78.1	27	130	6	21.66	0	0	5
Liverpool	2	3	0	26	14	8.66	0	0	40	9	105	2	52.50	0	0	0
Lord's	53	76	8	1523	113	22.39	2	7	1299.5	467	2717	119	22.83	2	0	34
Lydney	1	1	0	15	15	15.00	0	0	28.3	15	46	4	11.50	0	0	0
Maidstone	1	2	0	53	33	26.50	0	0	8	2	35	0	—	0	0	1
Manchester	22	28	6	624	107	28.36	1	2	499.5	187	956	42	22.76	3	0	13
Neath	1	2	0	19	19	9.50	0	0	36.4	17	61	2	30.50	0	0	0
Northampton	16	22	5	523	86	30.76	0	3	410.2	175	771	63	12.23	5	0	12
Nottingham	23	30	7	600	97	26.08	0	3	467.3	161	1011	36	28.08	1	0	11
Oxford	12	9	2	149	44*	21.28	0	0	266.3	107	519	27	19.22	1	0	8
Portsmouth	4	7	3	196	86*	49.00	0	1	64	26	148	5	29.60	0	0	6
Romford	2	3	1	13	7*	6.50	0	0	22	3	56	0	—	0	0	0
Southampton	2	4	0	30	15	7.50	0	0	50.5	8	143	7	20.42	0	0	2
Southend	3	4	0	125	116	31.25	1	0	24.4	5	76	5	15.20	0	0	2
Swansea	8	13	4	179	42*	19.88	0	0	290	108	632	52	11.10	5	1	5
Taunton	11	14	2	262	79	21.83	0	1	191.2	63	437	22	19.86	0	0	4
The Oval	27	45	7	762	127	20.05	1	3	902.2	308	1948	83	23.46	4	1	19
Torquay	4	7	0	47	23	6.71	0	0	111	26	370	22	16.81	3	0	6
Tunbridge Wells	2	3	0	33	29	11.00	0	0	52	18	134	12	11.16	1	0	2
Westcliff	1	2	0	41	39	20.50	0	0	32	14	54	1	54.00	0	0	0
Worcester	13	20	6	535	58	38.21	0	3	334	119	655	32	19.50	1	1	4
Worksop	3	4	0	41	22	10.25	0	0	74.1	30	142	8	17.75	1	0	4
Totals	356	509	86	10910	150	25.79	10	45	8968.2	3245	18844	955	19.73	43	5	217

YORKSHIRE AND BACK

GROUNDS – SUMMARY

	M	Inns	NO	Runs	HS	Avge	100s	50s	Overs	Mdns	Runs	Wkts	Avge	5 in Inns	10 in Mtch	Ct
In Yorkshire	255	354	72	8388	162	29.74	7	40	6408.5	2344	13875	769	18.04	45	4	143
In Leicestershire	100	129	38	3377	153*	37.10	4	16	2501	831	5153	254	20.28	16	2	50
Others in UK	356	509	86	10910	150	25.79	10	45	8968.2	3245	18844	955	19.73	43	5	217
Totals – UK	711	992	196	22675	162	28.48	21	101	17878.1	6420	37872	1978	19.14	104	11	410
In Australia	20	30	7	727	65*	31.60	0	3	†429.5	94	1392	32	43.50	0	0	9
In New Zealand	6	7	0	139	46	19.85	0	0	†41 / 50	33	200	5	40.00	0	0	7
In South Africa	4	6	2	83	31	20.75	0	0	86	23	240	5	48.00	0	0	3
In West Indies	12	16	2	353	100	25.21	1	2	365	107	781	11	71.00	0	0	3
Totals – Overseas	42	59	11	1302	100	27.12	1	5	†470.5 / 501	257	2613	53	49.30	0	0	22
Totals	753	1051	207	23977	162	28.40	22	106	†470.5 / 18379.1	6677	40485	2031	19.93	104	11	432

HOW HE WAS OUT

Caught	489	(58.0%)
Bowled	183	(21.7%)
LBW	133	(15.8%)
Stumped	23	(2.7%)
Run Out	13	(1.5%)
Hit Wicket	2	(0.2%)
Retired Out	1	(0.1%)
Total	844	(100.0%)

HOW HE TOOK HIS WICKETS

Caught	1158	(57.0%)
Bowled	583	(28.7%)
LBW	214	(10.6%)
Stumped	74	(3.6%)
Hit Wicket	2	(0.1%)
Total	2031	(100.0%)

RESULTS AS CAPTAIN

	Captained	Won	Lost	Drawn
FOR ENGLAND	31	12	5	14
FOR YORKSHIRE	4	2	1	1
FOR LEICESTERSHIRE	175	56	32	87
FOR OTHER TEAMS	18	6	7	5
	228	76 (33.3%)	45 (19.7%)	107 (47.0%)

ONE-DAY CRICKET

	M	Inns	NO	Runs	HS	Avge	50s	Overs	Mdns	Runs	Wkts	Avge	5 in Inns	Ct
ONE-DAY INTERNATIONALS	2	1	0	4	4	4.00	0	11	1	34	1	34.00	0	1
GILLETTE CUP:														
For Yorkshire	10	8	5	148	45	49.33	0	46	4	121	7	17.28	1	5
For Leicestershire	19	19	4	224	59	14.93	1	161	25	497	13	38.23	0	4
Totals Gillette Cup	29	27	9	372	59	20.66	1	207	29	618	20	30.90	1	9
JOHN PLAYER LEAGUE For Leicestershire	117	75	26	1433	79	29.24	3	591	52	2335	88	26.53	1	26
BENSON AND HEDGES CUP For Leicestershire	33	28	11	485	43*	28.52	0	296.1	56	881	40	22.02	1	9
TOTALS – ONE-DAY MATCHES	181	131	46	2294	79	26.98	4	1105.1	138	3868	149	25.95	3	45